THE LOST ART OF MEDITATION

BY
JOHN WILMOT MAHOOD

Published by Left of Brain Books

Copyright © 2021 Left of Brain Books

ISBN 978-1-396-32249-5

First Edition

All rights reserved. No part of this publication may be reproduced, distributed, or transmitted in any form or by any means, including photocopying, recording, or other electronic or mechanical methods, without the prior written permission of the publisher, except in the case of brief quotations embodied in critical reviews and certain other noncommercial uses permitted by copyright law. Left of Brain Books is a division of Left of Brain Onboarding Pty Ltd.

Table of Contents

FOREWORD	1
I. MEDITATION AND PRAYER	3
II. MEDITATION AND SOUL DEVELOPMENT	9
III. MEDITATION AND NATURE	13
IV. MEDITATION AND THE INTELLECTUAL LIFE	20
V. MEDITATION AND REVELATION	24
VI. MEDITATION AND CALVARY	29
VII. MEDITATION AND THE BIBLE	34
VIII. MEDITATION AND PREACHING	39
IX. MEDITATION AND WORSHIP	45
X. MEDITATION AND RESERVE POWER	51
XI. MEDITATION AND SOUL WINNING	56
XII. MEDITATION AND VISION	60
XIII. MEDITATION AND ACTION	67
XIV. HELPS TO MEDITATION	71

FOREWORD

SHALL we say it is a *lost art*—this withdrawal within the veil? Shall we say that this busy, restless age thinks it has outgrown the need for listening to the voice that speaks only to the soul? That saintly mystic, John Tauler, said that one might learn more in one short hour from the inward voice than from man in a thousand years, and if he had reference to the deep things of God he was probably right. Yet in these days how little time the average Christian gives to the inward look and the inward voice.

Now religion is both a science and an art. In recent years much attention has been given to the scientific side. The age has been one of discovery—discovery in mechanics, in astronomy, in therapeutics, in social economics. This spirit of exploration has also extended into the realm of religion. And this is well. The Church of Jesus Christ owes much to the patient investigation carried on by men of great devotion to the interests of the kingdom of God. But it must not be forgotten that while science discovers, art creates. In our enthusiasm for the discovery side of religion it is possible to forget the creative side. The art of Christian character building has been much neglected, and where this is neglected it is so easy to allow ourselves to drift on the tide of worldliness and spiritual indifference. We need a renaissance in the art of Christian living.

In this intensely practical and explorative age we have gone to the opposite extreme from the mystical and contemplative. Indeed so little time is given to meditation that it may well be called a lost art. We have no longer time to ponder the great truths of life and destiny. With breathless haste we rush after something new among the things of time and sense, and leave no room or strength for the hour of contemplation.

"Meditation," said Rodriguez, "is the beginning and ground of all good. It is the sister of spiritual reading, the nurse of prayer, and the director of good actions. It causes true devotion to spring up in our hearts. It is that which, next to the grace of God, most of all warms the heart and the will, and produces the prompt disposition to do virtuous deeds."

Haste and worry are anything but helpful to that purest devotion and loftiest thought which are essential in the making of character. He who sees God's mountains from the window of the speeding express train, or from the thronging streets of mountain cities, will never see their real glory. One must stand alone in the vast solitudes surrounded by snow-capped giants and let the mountains grow on him to experience the soul touch of majesty. And he who would know God must be much alone with God.

What means this low tone of Christian experience, and this shallow, self-satisfied profession of religion? What means this thoughtless, irreverent, jocular way of speaking of holy things, so prevalent to-day? Has not the hurry and fever of this busy age crowded out the time for meditation and prayer? We have been too busy to wait in the inner chamber with God, and we have lost soul poise and cloudless vision. Our minds have not felt the grip of eternal verities, nor have we bathed our souls in the pure white light that streams from the Shekinah of His secret presence.

J. W. M.

Sioux City, Iowa.

I.

MEDITATION AND PRAYER

But thou, when thou prayest, enter into thine inner chamber, and having shut thy door, pray to thy Father who is in secret, and thy Father who seeth in secret shall recompense thee.
—*Jesus.*

WHEN that old philosopher, Aristotle, saw dimly the light that leads to God and declared that there was one path open to the Eternal—the way of contemplation—it was a foregleam, of the true Christian's highest privilege—intimate and direct communion with God.

"No one becomes perfect on a sudden," said an old writer; "it is by mounting, and not flying, that we come to the top of the ladder. Let us therefore ascend, and let meditation and prayer be the two feet we make use of to do so. For meditation lets us see our wants, and prayer obtains for us relief from God. The one makes us discern the dangers that surround us; the other gives us happy escape from them. Prayer is tepid without meditation."

Some of the mystics taught that the contemplative life was a spiritual stage to which only a few could attain. It was an experience for pinnacle moments, they said, when the soul stands in God's presence with unveiled face. But the New Testament teaching would certainly indicate that every child of God may live the life of sweet and blessed fellowship provided the mind is stayed on Him. "Within my heart is the eternal adoration," said the saintly Tersteegen, reminding us of the Apostle's words, "Pray without ceasing. In everything give thanks: for this is the will of God in Christ Jesus concerning you." To have formed the habit of prayer, or to be always in the spirit of prayer, or in soul touch with God is, according to Paul, the privilege of every Christian.

Now this high privilege cannot be obtained or maintained save as meditation is joined with prayer. Meditation upon the word of God, upon the goodness of God, upon the providence of God, quickens the desire for prayer and gives life and power to prayer. No matter how frail the physical life, or how humble the social life, meditation will bring the prayer life to its full bloom.

What gave Catherine of Sienna her power? There was no helpful environment in her early life. She was the youngest of twenty-five children and the daughter of a wool dyer. She had very few social and educational advantages. Her own father tried to force her to live a worldly life. But in her hours of meditation God became her teacher. The Spirit unfolded the higher things of life in such a way that when she came to womanhood she was sought for by kings and queens and popes and princes that they might have her advice and her prayers. She went in person to Avignon and persuaded the vacillating pope to return to Rome. She rebuked him for his neglect of the spiritual interests of the church. She wrote Gregory XI thus: "Temporal things are failing you from no other cause than from your neglect of the spiritual. . . . I wish and pray that the moment of time that remains (for you) be dealt with manfully, following Christ, whose vicar you are, like a strong man." Whence had this woman of lowly birth and meagre educational advantages this power to rebuke sinners in high places? No one who studies her marvellous life can fail to conclude that the secret of it all lay in her habit of meditation and prayer. She was the friend of God. She believed herself to be the espoused of the King of heaven; and believed too that she had received the *stigmata*—the imprint of the five wounds of Christ.

Meditation is indispensable to prevailing prayer. The greatest and best men the world has ever known have cultivated the habit of withdrawing from the world to look into their own hearts and to let God speak to them in the secret place. When the distractive noises of the world are hushed then God's voice is heard more plainly, and the vision of His presence is seen more clearly. When Moses was alone in the desert he saw the flaming acacia tree and heard the voice of God when Jacob was alone by Jabbok's brook the angel of the Lord drew near and gave him a new name. It is through the portals of silence that we must pass to meet God face to face.

Said the saintly Fenelon, "Do not devote all your time to action, but reserve a certain portion of it for meditation upon eternity. We see Jesus Christ inviting His disciples to go apart, in a desert place, and rest a while, after their return from the cities, where they had been to announce His religion. How much more necessary is it for us to approach the source of all virtue, that we may revive our declining faith and charity, when we return from the busy scenes of life, where men speak and act as if they had never known that there is a God!"

Now prayer waits upon reverence. Indeed, where there is little reverence there is usually little prayer. To pray well one must be deeply reverent. But meditation upon the great truths and great works of God is essential to reverence. "Meditate on great things," said William Law, "and your soul will grow great." The surest indication of littleness of soul may be seen in disrespect for sacred things. "How shameful," said Saint Francis, "to allow oneself to fall into vain distractions when one is addressing the Great King. We should not speak in that manner even to a respectable man."

Prayer waits upon thoughtfulness. How thoughtlessly we often rush into the presence of the King of kings! How little preparation of heart and mind we sometimes make for audience with the eternal God! In the "Saints' Everlasting Rest," that classic of devotional literature, the author has this to say concerning reverence in our approach to God: "Be sure you set upon this work with great solemnity of heart and mind. There is no trifling in holy things. 'God will be sanctified in them that come nigh Him.' Labour, therefore, to have the deepest apprehensions of the presence of God, and His incomprehensible greatness. If Queen Esther must not draw near 'until the king hold out the sceptre,' think, then, with what reverence thou shouldest approach Him, who made the worlds with the word of His mouth, who upholds the earth as in the palm of His hand, who keeps the sun, moon, and stars in their courses, and who sets bounds to the raging sea! Thou art going to converse with Him, before whom the earth will quake and devils do tremble, and at whose bar thou and all the world must shortly stand, and be finally judged. . . . Labour also to apprehend the greatness of the work which thou attemptest, and to be deeply sensible both of its importance and excellency. If thou wast pleading for thy life at the bar of an earthly judge thou wouldst be serious, and yet that would be a trifle to this. If thou wast engaged in such a work as David against Goliath, on which the welfare of a kingdom depended, in itself, it were nothing to this. Suppose thou wast going to such a wrestling as Jacob's, or to see the sight which the three disciples saw in the mount, how seriously, how reverently, wouldst thou both approach and behold! If but an angel from heaven should appoint to meet thee, at the same time and place of thy contemplations, with what dread wouldst thou be filled? Consider, then, with what a spirit thou shouldst meet the Lord, and with what seriousness and awe thou shouldst daily converse with Him."

Prayer waits upon faith. That attitude of will and heart towards God whereby we find it easy to take that which God Faith has promised can only be attained by meditation upon the goodness and faithfulness of God. Faith claims; faith takes. John MacNeil used to say, "If a man has a credit balance of two hundred and fifty dollars in his banking account, and draws a check for fifty dollars, he does not need to go to the cashier and ask for fifty dollars; he presents his check and claims it, for it is his own. When God gives the Christian a definite promise it is the Christian's privilege to *claim, to receive* the thing promised."

The two greatest dangers to which we are constantly exposed in these days is a lost sense of sin, and a lost sense of God. It is so easy to be influenced by certain modern ideas of sin, and to think of it as mere "embryonic goodness," or "righteousness in state of formation," or "an hallucination of the mortal mind," until sin loses all its heinousness, and then Calvary all its merit. Meditation and prayer will develop a sensitiveness to sin and a consciousness of its awfulness. Richard Baxter, after months of meditation upon the calamity of sin, wrote: "You can never know the evil, nor the desert of sin, until you know

"1. The excellency of the soul which it deformeth.
2. The excellency of the holiness which it obliterates.
3. The reason and excellency of the law it violates.
4. The excellency of the glory it despises.
5. The excellency and office of reason which it treadeth down.
6. The infinite excellency, almightiness, and holiness of that God against whom it is committed."

Only meditation and prayer will develop a sense of the reality and immanence of God. The soul comes face to face with the Eternal. The heavens are no longer empty; and life is no longer a mere dream life to the man of prayer. Wherever he goes he bears upon his face the consciousness of heavenly companionship. If any man has a right to speak at this point it is surely John Bunyan, the immortal dreamer. He has this to say: "It is a great thing to be a closet-Christian, and to hold it; he must be a close-Christian that will be a closet-Christian. When I say a close-Christian, I mean one that is so in the hidden part, and that also walks with God. Many there be that profess Christ, who do oftener frequent the coffee house than their closet; and that sooner in a morning run to make bargains than to pray unto God and begin the day with Him. But for thee, who professest the name of Christ, do thou depart from all these things; do thou make conscience of reading and practicing; do thou follow after righteousness; do thou make conscience of beginning the day with God. For he that begins it not with Him will hardly end it with Him; he that runs from God in the morning will hardly find Him at the close of the day; nor will he that begins with the world and the vanities thereof be very capable of walking with God all the day after. It is he that finds God in his closet that will carry the savour of Him into his house, his shop, and his more open conversation. When Moses had been with God in the mount his face shone; he brought of that glory into the camp."

It has been said that our great need to-day is more prayer. But it must be the prayer that is joined to meditation if it prevails. Such prayer will be intercessory. Such prayer will be mighty. This is an age of vast opportunity for the Church of Christ. Everywhere fields are white unto harvest. At home and abroad there is need of a great army of workers. And, to be equal to the opportunities of so many needy fields, they must be men of unshakeable convictions and mighty in prayer. If there would come to our churches and colleges and homes a great revival of intercessory prayer how speedily the kingdom of our Lord and Saviour would triumph! To the secret place of meditation and prayer let us hasten then that we may have that preparation of the inner life that will make us mighty for God.

A Meditation

My soul, practice being alone with Christ! It is written that "when they were alone He expounded all things to His disciples." Do not wonder at the saying; it is true to thine experience. If thou wouldst understand *thyself* send the multitude away. Let them go out one by one till thou art left alone with

Jesus. . . . Hast thou ever pictured thyself the one remaining creature in the earth, the one remaining creature in all the starry worlds? In such a universe thine every thought would be "God and I! God and I!" And yet He is as near to thee as that—as near as if in the boundless spaces there throbbed no heart but His and thine. Practice that solitude, O my soul! Practice the expulsion of the crowd! Practice the stillness of thine own heart! Practice the solemn refrain "God and I! God and I!" Let none interpose between thee and thy wrestling angel! Thou shalt be both condemned and pardoned when thou shalt meet Jesus alone!

—*George Matheson.*

II.

MEDITATION AND SOUL DEVELOPMENT

> There is nothing that makes men rich and strong but that which they carry inside of them. Wealth is of the heart, not of the hand.
> —*John Milton.*

SAID Robert Browning in his introduction to "Sordello," "My stress lay on the incidents in the development of a soul: little else is worth study." This reminds us of what Socrates says in his "Apology": "For I do nothing but go about persuading you all, old and young alike, not to take thought for your persons, or your properties, but first and chiefly to care about the greatest improvement of the soul." What words are these for a time like this! We are still covered with the grime of this materialistic age through which we have been passing, and need the uplifting and cleansing power of a new ideal if we would bring to their richest fruitage the heaven-born powers of these immortal souls. "The path of the just is as the shining light that shineth more and more unto the perfect day." There must be soul development if there would be spiritual manhood as surely as there must be bodily development if there would be physical manhood.

Now in the realm of Biblical study we have higher criticism; in the realm of astronomy we have the higher mathematics; in the realm of mental training we have the higher education; in the realm of spiritual culture why not have the *higher athletics?* Ignatius wrote to Polycarp and said, "Watch as God's athlete"; and Paul writing to Timothy speaks of a "gymnastic unto godliness."

In the realm of economics we may say that our own country leads the world; in the realm of politics we may think that she holds first place among the nations; in Olympic games our physical supremacy may have been demonstrated. But what are we profited if in economics, and politics, and muscular development the world's primacy belongs to us, if in morals and spiritual understanding we are wanting? The development of the body is necessary to the highest manhood provided that development does not interfere with the growth of the entire nature. But to be a Swaboda in the realm of the physical and a Mark Hopkins in the realm of the intellectual, and a pigmy in the realm of the spiritual, is to be a monstrosity rather than a man.

Robert Browning loved to make life one great Olympic game where spiritual athletes contended for supremacy. His hero was one who never turned his back but marched breast forward:

> "Never doubted clouds would break,
> Never dreamed though right was worsted, right would triumph,
> Held we fall to rise, are baffled to fight better, Sleep to wake."

Now God has provided means for the development of every faculty of the spiritual nature. There is a spiritual gymnasium for God's athletes. The equipment is complete. The inner life may be symmetrically and fully developed but not without effort. "Let us give diligence," said the writer of that treatise on spiritual athletics, "to enter into that rest;" "Let us run with patience the race that is set before us looking unto Jesus, the file leader;" and again "Let us press on unto perfection."

Among those things that are necessary to spiritual mastery meditation has a large place. We must often look within to know our need. Meditation will create soul hunger. All our spiritual lameness and blindness and nakedness will appear in the quiet of the inner chamber. Then there will come into the life a great unrest to be satisfied only in Christ. We will want to fly to Him who said, "Come unto Me all ye that labour and are heavy laden, and I will give you rest."

Meditation will aid *physical mastery*. The highest soul development will come only after we have, by the grace of God, brought the physical nature into subjection. The body must be kept under perfect control if we would live at our best. Paul was concerned for this and he said, "I buffet my body, and bring it into bondage: lest by any means, after that I have preached to others, I myself should be rejected." He said, too, "Know ye not that your bodies are members of Christ... glorify God therefore in your body." Meditation is not dreaming. Meditation is not for the spirit only, nor for the mind only; it is for the whole man. Meditation will help open every window of the life to the Light from heaven, and that means that every power of the consecrated body and mind and spirit shall be quickened and strengthened. We must, by the grace of God, keep the physical in subjection to the spiritual, for we are essentially spiritual beings. Meditation will help us to a right estimate of the relation between body and soul, and give us to see more clearly that our bodies are temples of the Holy Spirit.

Meditation will give *power of vision*. Nothing is more important to soul growth. To have the vision that apprehends God, and sees all things in their true relation to God, is worth striving for. Indeed to fail here is to fail in all things that are worth while. "Where there is no vision the people perish." These are days of narrow vision. Some fix their eyes upon one principle of nature, or one law of life, or one doctrine of the Word of God, and seem to see nothing else. Would to God that we might have the vision that is high enough and wide enough to see that there is a whole universe of truth constantly unfolding. Would to God that we might have a vision clear enough to see over our own little prejudices and notions, and gain the world view. To many the greatest things in life are so vague and shadowy as to seem almost unreal, because of a lack of spiritual vision. Meditation will develop the inner life. It will take the veil off the face of reason. When united with a living faith it will help us see the things of the soul life in their true perspective. It is when prayerful meditation has its place in daily life that

> "Faith lends its realizing light,
> The clouds disperse, the shadows flee;
> The invisible appears in sight,
> And God is seen by mortal eye."

Meditation will encourage the spirit of *praise and thanksgiving*. This, too, is essential to soul growth. Goethe's mother used to say that when her son had a grief he turned it into a poem and so got rid of it. If we could always turn our griefs into songs how soon they would be forgotten. And until we lose our worry and heart disquiet in some symphony of praise there can never be rapid spiritual progress. The hurry and rush of modern life has crowded out everything save that which is intensely practical, and praise is not supposed to be practical. But here is where we blunder. Praise is the most practical thing in human life. We were created to praise and glorify God. Life's highest efficiency can never be reached until we fulfill the purpose of our creation.

Then only can there be real soul development. Praise is life's halo, and it was Susan Ferrier who said, "My deepest wish is that life may never lose its halo." It must be kept bright and glowing through constant meditation on the goodness of God.

"Solitude," said Cecil, "is my great ordinance." There are heaven-born gifts and powers in our lives of which we will never be conscious until in solitude they are revealed and developed. Look at John Bunyan. Did not Bedford jail bring out the best that was in him? Look at John Milton. Did not sightless eyes reveal glories he would otherwise never have seen? Look at David Livingstone. Those eight or nine years in the solitudes of Africa during his early missionary career prepared him as nothing else could have done for the remarkable series of explorations and victories that resulted in opening a continent to Christ. Or look at Paul the Apostle. From a Roman dungeon Paul gave us his best. Because Paul was a prisoner at Rome what wealth of spiritual teaching, and what glimpses of the unseen and eternal are ours! There his life came to its richest fruitage. And earthly life for us will only reach its highest bliss, and these heaven-born faculties their fullest fruition when we are much alone with God.

A Hymn

Be strong!
We are not here to play, to dream, to drift,
We have hard work to do, and loads to lift.
Shun not the struggle, face it, 'tis God's gift.

Be strong!
Say not the days are evil—who's to blame?
And fold the hands and acquiesce—O shame!
Stand up, speak out, and bravely, in God's name.

Be strong!
It matters not how deep intrenched the wrong,
How hard the battle goes, the day, how long;
Faint not, fight on! To-morrow comes the song.

—Maltbie D. Babcock.

III.

MEDITATION AND NATURE

> I meditate on all Thy doings:
> I muse on the work of Thy hands.
> —*David.*

> "God is the perfect Poet
> Who in creation acts His own conception."

IT is only when with reverent and prayerful hearts we consider the glory of His works that we can read God's poem of nature. If one has the open eye and the clean heart he can say with Kipling,

> "It is enough that through Thy grace
> I saw naught common on the earth."

There is nothing common to the man who has a vision of nature. Earth, and sea, and sky are full of wonder and majesty.

> "Earth's crammed with heaven
> And every common bush afire with God;
> But only he who sees takes off his shoes."

There is a sacramental glory in the humblest object of God's care and providence. "Consider the lilies of the field, how they grow; they toil not, neither do they spin: yet I say unto you, that Solomon in all his glory was not arrayed like one of these." Joseph Parker was surely inspired when he wrote: "The meanest insect that flutters in the warm sunlight is a grander thing than the proudest marble statue ever chiselled by the proudest sculptor." Linnæus, the great scientist, saw a little flower unfolding, and said, "I saw God in His glory passing before me and I bowed my head in worship;" and Carlyle wrote, "One may look through a small window and see the Infinite."

As the words of the book express the mind of the writer, so do the wonders of nature express the mind of God, and create in the reverent and loving heart a song of praise. Thus it was with St. Francis of Assisi who, as he journeyed with his companions up and down the lovely vale of Umbria, sang his Canticle of the Sun, declared by Renan to be "the most perfect utterance of modern religious sentiment." It came from a heart thrilled with the beauties of nature, and glowing with exultant praise. Translated by Matthew Arnold it runs as follows:

"Oh, most high, almighty, good Lord God, to Thee belong praise, honour, and blessing!

"Praised be my Lord God with all His creatures, and specially our brother the sun, who brings us the day and who brings us the light; fair is he and shines with a very great splendour. Oh, Lord, he signifies to us Thee!

"Praised be my Lord for our sister the moon, and for the stars the which He has set clear and lovely in the heaven.

"Praised be my Lord for our brother the wind, and for air and for clouds, calms and all weather by which Thou upholdest life in all Thy creatures.

"Praised be my Lord for our sister water, who is very serviceable unto us and humble and precious and clean.

"Praised be my Lord for our brother fire, through whom Thou givest us light in the darkness; and he is bright and pleasant and very mighty and strong.

"Praised be my Lord for our mother the earth, the which doth sustain and keep us, and bringeth forth divers fruits, and flowers of many colours, and grass.

"Praised be my Lord for all those who pardon one another for His love's sake, and who endure weakness and tribulation blessed are they who peaceably shall endure, for Thou, oh Most Highest, shalt give them a crown.

"Praised be my Lord for our sister, the death of the body, from which no man escapeth. Woe to him who dieth in mortal sin! Blessed are they who are found walking by Thy most holy will, for the second death shall have no power to do them harm.

"Praise ye and bless the Lord, and give thanks unto Him, and serve Him with great humility."

How few there are in this restless age, even among Christian people, who stop to meditate upon the handiwork of God. So many have eyes but see not.

Even where nature is most prodigal in her beauty men seem not to see. Under the shadow of those great snow-crowned peaks in the Rocky Mountains I found men who seemed to have no appreciation of the majesty all about them. With their hearts and eyes upon gold and pleasure they exist in God's beautiful world more like the beasts of the field than like God-created and God-endowed men. A poor artist said to a coarse rich man: "When the sun rises you see something like a golden guinea coming out of the sea. I see, and hear likewise, something like an innumerable company of angels praising God."

Meditation upon the glories of nature *will bring heaven near to earth, and make spiritual things seem more real.* The every-day things of life will take on new interest, and the soul will be able to interpret nature as the revelation of the Divine. I stood on the eastern shore of a beautiful lake, set like a gem in the heart of one of our great states, and saw the sun descend towards the western horizon, surrounded by draperies of cloud that seemed to spread themselves out like the ramparts of a mighty city. Then it seemed to me as I stood and looked that I could see domes of amethyst and gates of pearl and walls of jasper and streets of gold. It was as if the City of God itself had come down to earth; and the slanting rays of the setting sun on the shimmering waters of the lake made a shining pathway that led straight to the City of Light. And there is scarcely a day that passes but one may see in sunrise and sunset, in field and forest, in snowflake and dewdrop, in mountain and valley, in seashore and ocean the majesty of the King.

Meditation upon nature, when coupled with the grace of God in the heart, will bring *a holy quiet and confidence.* The peacefulness of flower and field and sky will pass into the life. Wordsworth tells how nature transforms the life of one who meditates on its beauty and glory:

> "She shall lean her ear
> In many a secret place
> Where rivulets dance their wayward round,
> And beauty born of murmuring sound
> Shall pass into her face."

It was Wordsworth's vision of God in nature that gave him that remarkable gift of glorifying the common things of every day. It was no illusion, as Matthew Arnold would have us believe, but a real insight into the majesty and glory of that which God had made. Through meditation on nature he had come to a true conception of nature. He saw that all things shared the life of God. Whittier, in that beautiful appreciation of Wordsworth, expresses it clearly:

> The violet by its mossy stone,
>   The primrose by the river's brim,
> And chance sown daffodil have found
>   Immortal life through him.
>
> The sunrise on his breezy lake,
>   The rosy tints his sunset brought,
> World seen, are gladdening all the vales
>   And mountain peaks of thought.
>
> Art builds on sand; the works of pride
>   And human passion change and fall;
> But that which shares the life of God
>   With him surviveth all.

Meditation on nature will give us new confidence in the *faithfulness of God*. The promise made to Noah will have a new meaning: "While the earth remaineth, seed-time and harvest, and cold and heat, and summer and winter, and day and night shall not cease." We shall then see with the psalmist that the days and the nights have voices:

> "Day unto day uttereth speech,
>   And night unto night showeth knowledge."

God will speak to the inquiring heart in a multitude of ways:

> "To him who in the love of nature holds
>   Communion with her visible forms, God speaks
> A various language."

The flowers will speak God's messages to us—not in the English, or the French, or the German tongue, but in the language of beauty and design and delicacy of tracery. The stars, too, will have voices, and the heavens will declare the glory of God:

> "What though in solemn silence all
> Move round the dark terrestrial ball;
> What though no real voice nor sound
> Amid their radiant orbs be found;
> In reason's ear they all rejoice
> And utter forth a glorious voice;
> Forever singing as they shine,
> The hand that made us is Divine."

All nature will remind us that we have a covenant keeping God, and He who cares for and clothes the lilies of the field will surely take care of us for whom He made the lilies.

Meditation on nature will give us a new conception of the *power of God*. A reverent study of the great forces of electricity and gravitation and chemical affinity should bring into the life a new consciousness of the presence of an omnipotent God. The smallest things in life will have a new interest if we see God's power unveiled in them. Sir Oliver Lodge says that if a dewdrop were expanded to the size of a planet the molecules of hydrogen, of which it consists, would resemble oranges or footballs; and now scientists tell us that within each molecule is a stellar system which is an almost exact reproduction of our solar system, and that all we find in the planets, both as to their orbits and their speed, we find in the flying electrons of an invisible atom of matter.

Then, too, who can meditate on the glory and majesty of the heavens as revealed in these later days through the medium of telescope and spectroscope and photographic lens, without having a new vision of the power of God? Look, for instance, at that wonderful group of worlds known to us as the Pleiades. Only seven or eight are visible to the naked eye. But we now know that there are nearly three thousand suns in that beautiful constellation. And we know, too, that such infinite distances separate some of these blazing suns that it takes light at least three or four years to go from one pleiad to another. Alcyone—the brightest of the group—gives out twenty-four hundred times more light than our sun, and is sixty times more brilliant than Sirius. Such is the glory and majesty of that mighty sun that when the great scientist, Mäedler, studied it through the telescope he declared that it was the centre of the universe, the seat of the Eternal, the throne of God. Lord Kelvin declared that there were at least one thousand million suns scattered through space, many of them much larger than our sun. Who can think of the mighty forces that must control and preserve these myriad worlds without an overwhelming consciousness of the power of our God?

Meditation on nature will give a new appreciation of the *holiness of God*. In these days we are in danger of losing sight of the holiness of God. We think of God's omnipotence and omnipresence and omniscience and forget about His holiness. Perhaps this is the reason why many have come to think lightly of sin. Dean Church said: "This deep austere note of religion runs like an undertone through all the Old Testament, and the New. The Christian does not shudder at mere omnipotence. But he bows his head and worships the unutterable holiness of the Father." To have the vision of God's holiness is to cry out like Isaiah, "Woe is me for I am undone," or like Peter, "Depart from me for I am a sinful man." But that cry, when from the depths of the heart, always brings peace and gives, new zest to life.

What a freshness and interest all life would have if we knew that in flaming letters on every leaf and flower and blade of grass were written the words, "Holy, Holy, Holy, Lord God Almighty!" But to the meditative soul they are written there. Not in the Latin of the text-books to be sure, but in the language of design and beauty. Every flower is "God's angel of the grass," and every clover blossom is an amethyst to him who, like Enoch of old, walks with God.

A Hymn

>Still, still with Thee, when purple morning breaketh,
>   When the bird waketh, and the shadows flee;
>Fairer than morning, lovelier than daylight,
>   Dawns the sweet consciousness, I am with Thee.
>
>Alone with Thee, amid the mystic shadows,
>   The solemn hush of nature newly born;
>Alone with Thee in breathless adoration,
>   In the calm dew and freshness of the morn.
>
>As in the dawning o'er the waveless ocean,
>   The image of the morning star doth rest,

So in this stillness, Thou beholdest only
    Thine image in the waters of my breast.

Still, still to Thee! as to each newborn morning,
    A fresh and solemn splendour still is given,
So does this blessed consciousness awaking,
    Breathe each day nearness unto Thee and heaven.

When sinks the soul, subdued by toil, to slumber,
    Its closing eyes look up to Thee in prayer;
Sweet the repose beneath Thy wings o'ershading,
    But sweeter still, to wake and find Thee there.

So shall it be at last, in that bright morning,
    When the soul waketh, and life's shadows flee;
Oh, in that hour, fairer than daylight dawning,
    Shall rise the glorious thought—I am with Thee.

—Harriet B. Stowe.

IV.

MEDITATION AND THE INTELLECTUAL LIFE

> By all means use sometimes to be alone.
>   Salute thyself: see what thy soul doth wear.
> Dare to look in thy chest; for 'tis thine own:
>   And tumble up and down what thou findest there.
> Who cannot rest till be good fellows finde,
> He breaks up house, turns out-of-doors his minde.
>   —*George Herbert.*

"KNOWLEDGE is power," is a trite saying glibly uttered by many. But that depends. There are some kinds of knowing that weaken and destroy the noblest in man. There is a way of acquiring knowledge that makes the "knowing" of little use to us. There are human sponges that absorb everything they touch. But their knowledge is of little or no practical value to them. Only that knowledge is power which can be used in the development of higher manhood and womanhood—*which can be used*—mark you. "A thing known," says a certain writer, "is a thing incorporated into the human personality and made spiritual." Knowledge, to be used effectively, must be made a part of the very life. This can be done only by meditation. When some great truth has taken hold of the inmost being, then knowledge is power. When the "I know" comes with the definiteness of a great conviction, which has seemed a real experience, then knowledge is power.

An old man, recalling some of the most interesting incidents of his early life, told how he had once heard Jenny Lind sing that beautiful aria from Handel's Messiah, "I Know that My Redeemer Liveth." Said he: "The 'I know' of that woman's voice has thrilled my life through all these years." That was musical knowledge with power. And when in any department of human achievement the "I know" of a great conviction thrills the life, then knowledge is power.

1. *Meditation on great themes will produce positiveness of conviction.* "One man with conviction is worth a hundred men with mere opinions," said John Stuart Mill. We have too many colourless opinions and too little real assurance to-day. Victor Hugo said of Queen Anne that no qualities of hers ever attained to virtue, and none to vice; which was another way of saying that she had no distinct and positive convictions. The man who is not settled in his thought concerning certain great principles and verities of life will be like a reed shaken with the wind. There will be no stability in his Christian life, and he will be the easy prey of every passing religious fad and fantasy. From this class come the people who are led captive by every silly adventuress of some new religion. They have not allowed the truths of God to take deep root in heart and mind and so are the ready victims of every false prophet. To compel the mind to dwell long on the great truths of God, until from every angle we get a glimpse of their majesty, will produce in the mind a positiveness of conviction that will give steadiness of faith and set our feet upon a rock.

2. *Meditation on great themes encourages intellectual vigour.* Christianity is ever an aid to the development of mind power. This accounts for the fact that so many of the great discoverers in the realm of scientific knowledge have been earnest Christians. When the mind dwells much on the great truths of God it will be all the keener to unlock the secrets of nature. "The wisdom of life," says an Oriental proverb, "is to throw a noose over the stars." Men are constantly seeking to unlock the secrets of the great cosmic forces. But the man who has taken time to commune with nature's God will have a distinct advantage. Nature's secrets will open more easily their fast-closed doors to him whose thoughts have been stirred by visions of the Infinite. It is in "Les Miserables" that we find this striking paragraph:

"Thought, meditation, prayer—these are great and mysterious radiations. Let us respect them. Whither go these mysterious irradiations of the soul? Into the darkness; that is to say, to the light."

Meditation on great themes means a surer mental grasp of the problems of every-day life. The darkness that so often perplexes will usually yield to quiet, prayerful thought. It is said that one of the greatest of English engineers, when confronted with some tremendous difficulty in his work, would shut himself up in his room and refuse to eat anything or see anybody. He would so abandon himself to serious thought concerning the problem in hand that in two or three days at most he would come forth serene and confident, walk to the spot, and give direction to the work. In this way he accomplished some almost impossible engineering feats, throwing bridges across impassable chasms, and tunnelling mountains that seemed to defy the skill of man. Prayerful meditation will mean intellectual quickening, and life's daily duties will be better done and more quickly done.

3. *Meditation on great themes will lead us to a better knowledge of ourselves.* It was Coleridge who said, "There is an art of which every man should be master, the art of reflection. By reflection alone can self-knowledge be obtained." There is no man more likely to be deceived concerning himself than the man of shallow thought. He who cultivates the daily habit of thinking on some great theme will soon find that the inner eye of the soul sees more clearly the soul's need. There is nothing more dangerous to high thinking than that subtle pride of intellect which keeps us from seeing our own frailty and ignorance. But when we shut ourselves up with some great and good thought our own littleness and weakness will be reflected by its pure light, and we will seek again the source of all true wisdom and love and power. Not until like Paul we can say, "But far be it from me to glory, save in the cross of our Lord Jesus Christ, through which the world hath been crucified unto me, and I unto the world," will there be real soul satisfaction and rest of heart.

4. *Meditation on great themes will often give to the life an undying influence.* It will project individuality through generations to come. Newell Dwight Hillis well says: "Moses will control all our jurists to-morrow because he spent forty years in the desert reflecting upon the principles of justice. Paul had the honour to fashion our political institutions because he gave twelve years of general preparation and three years of special application to the study of individual rights. Milton tells us that he spent four and thirty years of solitary and unceasing study in accumulating his material for a heroic poem that the world would not willingly let die. . . . Pasteur gave our generation much because for thirty years he isolated himself and got much to give."

The Church of God needs great intellectual leaders, men who will think through its great social problems, and be able to turn the consecrated life of the Church into the channels of highest service. We need men who will stand in advance of all the Church's activities and beckon us onward towards the paths that lead to the highest good. We need men who have more than a one-sided view of our many complex social conditions, men who are large enough in thought, and wide enough in sympathy, and Christly enough in life to see all sides of these great interests. Such men come only from the place of quiet waiting and meditation where the Holy Spirit touches heart and brain. And such men will leave, behind them an influence for good that will gather impetus with the circling years.

A Prayer

O Holy Spirit, teach me that "the fear of the Lord is the beginning of wisdom." I submit myself to Thy instruction. Thou canst unlock every treasure house of the intellect. Thou canst lead the way through every labyrinth of the great world's thought. Thou canst guide to the highest peaks of reason's wonderful realm. I would go to school to Thee, and let Thee teach me the higher wisdom. I cannot penetrate the deep things of nature and grace unless Thou dost open the eyes of my understanding and enlarge my soul. In the quiet of this secret place speak to me now words that shall waken every slumbering faculty of my heaven-born nature; and thus Thou wilt help me to live at my best for my Lord.

V.

MEDITATION AND REVELATION

> For now we see in a mirror, darkly; but then face to face: now I know in part; but then shall I know fully even as also I was fully known.
>
> —*Paul.*

THE march of true science is always forward towards the heights of revelation. There is no conflict between reason and faith, and never can be. They are comrades, but one is fleeter and stronger than the other and goes farther just as the microscope and telescope go farther than the naked eye so faith outruns and goes infinitely farther than reason. Or it might be said that faith is reason's telescope. So there is no conflict between science and revelation. They, too, are comrades, but one is always in advance. Just as surely as God's prophets have always been in advance of the people leading them on, so revelation has always beckoned to science.

And the spiritual will ever lead the natural. The nearer science approaches the goal of some definite knowledge concerning the mysteries of nature the more ready she will be to uncover her head and cry, "Great and marvellous are Thy works, O Lord God, the Almighty; righteous and true are Thy ways, Thou king of the ages."

There was a time when the atomic theory was considered the end of wisdom concerning matter. We had three conditions of matter—solid, liquid, and gaseous. But now we have radiant matter: now we have electrons with all their wonderful symmetry and ethereal energies. Now we have almost an exact reproduction of the solar system in the atom that only so recently was supposed to be indivisible. Now we know that the tiny and invisible electrons, in the curve of their orbits and the speed of their flight, rival the stars in their courses. Thus the more we know of the mysteries of nature, the more we know of the glory and power and majesty of God.

And every pathway of true knowledge leads towards the spiritual and thus towards light, and thus towards God. Modern psychology, for instance, is largely in a physiological stage yet. As psychological knowledge increases it will become more and more spiritually visioned. Many recent text-books on psychological phenomena go limping, for the writer has neglected to keep spiritual vision clear, or he has failed to see the intimate relationship of God-consciousness and soul-consciousness. The man who does not know his Lord intimately and lovingly can never be a trusted authority in psychology. He must first have been on the mount of revelation with the Master.

There are three or four events in the earthly life of Jesus that stand out with royal beauty and power. The Transfiguration is one of these, and is full of sublime spiritual teaching. Only a few days and then would come the cross with all its tragedy and suffering. And just before the storm of the world's hate and passion breaks upon the Son of God He stands here surrounded by five men—two representing His Church in heaven, and three representing His Church on earth; and lo! the veil of the mortal is parted and they behold His glory. But Luke says that He went up into the mountain to *pray*. The hour of meditation and prayer had become the hour of revelation. Meditation and communion always result in transfiguration.

1. Meditation with Jesus on the mount reveals the immanence of the spiritual world. So near did it seem to Peter to be the ideal of joy that his first thought was to stay there. "Let us make three tabernacles; one for Thee, and one for Moses, and one for Elijah." Heaven is not far from those who tarry on the mount with their Lord.

> "Not where the wheeling systems darken,
> And our benumbed conceiving soars;
> The drift of pinions, would we harken,
> Beats at our own clay shuttered doors.

How beautifully Richard Watson Gilder expressed the immanence of the spiritual. He was camping with some friends under the pine trees, and one summer evening they sat talking of the future and what it had in store for deathless souls when face to face with God. That night as the poet lay awake the pine branches above him seemed to be whispering among themselves and saying:

> "Heard'st thou these wanderers dreaming of a time
> When man more near the Eternal One shall climb;
> How like the new-born babe, that cannot tell
> The mother's arm that wraps it warm and well."

If every God-created sense of this immortal soul were wide awake, how real would become the eternal world, and how near God would be! Then would we realize the truth of the poet's words:

> "Closer to me than breathing,
> Nearer than hands and feet."

Who has not in moments of meditation and prayer caught a glimpse of opening gates? Who has not in the secret place of holy communion felt the rush of some white surging wave of emotion—a foretaste of the joy of the blessed? Sometimes it is as if some angel had touched this frail body and bade us look upward. It is in such a moment that the struggling soul is nerved anew for the conflict with sin. Were it not that God vouchsafes to lead us up into some mount of transfiguration now and then many of us would become utterly discouraged. Dr. Joseph Parker once said: "If we do not get back to visions, peeps into heaven, consciousness of the higher glory and the larger life, we shall lose our religion; our altar will be a bare stone, unblessed by visitant from heaven."

2. Meditation with Jesus on the mount reveals something of the glory of the spiritual body. Here were men who were once as we are—subject to all the weaknesses and diseases of this earthly life—yet now clothed in immortal youth. The mortal had given way to the immortal, the natural to the spiritual. And yet they retained their identity. They were still Moses and Elijah as truly as when they walked the earth. No longer encumbered with the gross body of flesh, but the earthly body transmuted into that glorious spiritual organism of ethereal mould and immortal beauty.

That the spiritual body shall be possessed of mighty strength seems evident. We are to be "as the angels," and David said, "Oh, ye His angels that excel in strength." To move from sphere to sphere with the speed of thought on His high errands of love and mercy and judgment would seem to be at least a part of the employment of the glorified. What must it be to be worthy to be entrusted by the King of kings with a mission similar to that of Moses and Elijah, or of the angel whom John saw in vision, who, with one foot on the sea and the other on the land, sware by Him that liveth forever and ever that time shall be no more.

Here we are prisoners of the flesh, here many of us suffer with pain every waking hour, here many go limping all their days, here many never know the sweet sense of sight or hearing, here many are burdened with the frailties of old age, here many suffer poverty and are burdened in body and mind. But what must it be to be free—eternally, gloriously free, and to be messengers of the King? What must it be to be one moment in the darkness and distress of great physical pain and the next forever beyond pain and sorrow, and dwelling in "a house not made with hands, eternal in the heavens," and worthy to have a part in the high ministries of the Eternal Throne! Surely this is a change not to be feared, but welcomed when our work is done. "Beloved, now are we the sons of God and it doth not yet appear what we shall be; but we know that, when He shall appear, we shall be like Him; for we shall see Him as He is."

Meditation with Jesus on the mount gives reality to the power and majesty of Christ. The disciples had seen the glory of His humanity. They had been reproved by Him, exhorted by Him, encouraged by Him. But as yet they had apparently little conception of His real glory. The reality of the presence of the Son of God with them they could not grasp.

How many there are to whom their Lord is a mere phantom! He has no real personality. They think of one who lived and died nineteen hundred years ago and they revere His memory. But of a living, present Lord and Saviour and Friend they seem to have no conception. This is the reason why there are so many church-members who are inactive in Christian work. To them Christ is a name, a memory; not a life, a power. There is no impelling influence of holy love in their hearts. Look at Savonarola. When he had only the form of religion he was content to stay in the convent. But when the Christ became a reality in his life then convent walls could not hold him. Florence soon heard the thunder tones of his voice, and trembled. With Christ we will dare go down from the mountain top to battle with demons. The reality of His presence and power will make heroes of the weakest of us, and "one will chase a thousand, and two put ten thousand to flight."

Here is the world's need to-day—*men who have seen their Lord*. The world can never expect much from those to whom Christ is a mere name or a vague conception. If the Church of this twentieth century would go forward with a confidence, born of holy waiting before God, to say to the lost multitudes, "We have seen the Lord," nothing could stay her conquering march.

Meditation with Jesus on the mount gives new faith in the supernatural. Here the disciples had a glimpse into supernatural another kingdom. Here was a sample of the heavenly kingdom, and what to them seemed unnatural when the Master talked about it now seemed perfectly natural in the moment of experience. They wanted to stay here. These are days when some men are trying to eliminate the supernatural from the Bible. They seek to explain away the miracles of the Old and New Testaments and discount all that is superhuman in the life of Christ. But such have never dwelt on the mount. He who dwells on the mountain of meditation with the glorified Lord will easily come to see that what is supernatural to us may be very natural to those in a little higher realm of being. Indeed he will become conscious of what is called the supernatural. For to be on the mount is to be in communion with the living Christ, and thus, as Paul expresses it, "we know Him and the power of His resurrection." To really know Christ and the power of His resurrection means the banishment of all doubt concerning the supernatural in religion.

A Prayer

Almighty God, teach us Thy greatness through Thy goodness, lest we be affrighted, and become as men in whom there is no strength. We would see Thy glory, but our eyes could not bear the light; may we therefore see Thy mercy, and become accustomed to the milder glory. Show us that Thy pity is great, that Thy love itself is glorious, and thus, little by little, as we are able to bear it, do Thou continue and complete the revelation of Thyself in our wondering and grateful hearts. Thou dost grow upon us like an increasing light continue so to do until there be in us no darkness at all, our whole life beautiful with the presence of Thy glory, cleansed and purified by the fire of Thy righteousness.

—Joseph Parker.

VI.

MEDITATION AND CALVARY

> But far be it from me to glory, save in the cross of our Lord Jesus Christ, through which the world hath been crucified unto me, and I unto the world.
>
> —Paul.

THERE is no dynamic like Calvary. There is no magnet like the story of the cross. Among all the glorious doctrines of the Word of God the atonement must ever maintain the primacy. It is the master truth of all Scripture. The apostles knew no other preaching than the preaching of the cross. They had only one theme—Christ and Him crucified—about which were grouped all other themes. "Be it far from me," said Paul, "to glory, save in the cross of our Lord Jesus Christ, through which the world hath been crucified unto me, and I unto the world."

We live in a day of lessening emphasis upon the preaching of the cross of Christ. We do not take time to meditate, as did the fathers, on the passion of our Lord, and so we lose our appreciation of its infinite meaning. Through neglect of Calvary we become afraid of Calvary. We are not willing to see its suffering lest we become partakers. Look at St. Catherine. She felt such keen distress for lost souls about her, that as she turned towards Calvary she cried, "Give me Thy promise, dear Lord, that Thou wilt save them!" Then it seemed to her that the Lord grasped her hand and gave her the promise; but as He did so she felt a sharp pain as if a nail had pierced her palm. In these days of psychological wisdom we speak lightly of an experience like this, and easily explain it away. But this is sure, St. Catherine knew her Lord as many of us do not know Him, and she shared with Him the passion for lost souls. If we would stop to look at Calvary and see the suffering Lamb of God we too might share His travail of soul for the lost.

The experience of St. Francis similar to that of St. Catherine, and is familiar to all students of so-called mystical literature. For weeks he had been recalling the scenes of the crucifixion. He had fasted and prayed with the memory of Calvary ever before him. Again and again he had read the story of the Passion until the love and suffering of the Saviour had burned itself into his heart. He had spent the night in prayer, when, with the rising sun, there came to him a wondrous vision:

"A seraph with outspread wings flew towards him from the edge of the horizon, and bathed his soul in raptures unutterable. In the centre of the vision appeared a cross, and the seraph was nailed upon it. When the vision disappeared, he felt sharp sufferings, mingled with ecstasy in the first moments. Stirred to the very depths of his being, he was anxiously asking the meaning of it all, when be perceived upon his body the *Stigmata* of the *Crucified*."

Come with me, ye redeemed by the blood, and see now your dying Lord. Come first to Gethsemane, where, in His agony, He lies prostrate on the cold ground. See Him sweat great drops of blood. Hear Him cry, "Father, if Thou be willing, remove this cup from Me: nevertheless not My will, but Thine, be done." This was the crisis in that titanic struggle with sin and death. From this moment the tide of battle surges towards the cross. Now let sin and death do their worst.

See, here they come! The torches are flashing through the trees. His own disciple leads the murderous mob. They surround him with fiendish glee, and Judas gives the kiss of betrayal. Then they drag Him from the Garden towards the city. But we shall never know all that He endured on that way of sorrow. Tissot, the great painter, represents them, while crossing the stone bridge over Kedron, pushing Him over the side of the bridge, and He falls prostrate in the bed of the brook below. There for a moment He may lave His feverish lips in the cooling waters, thus fulfilling an old prophecy, "He shall drink of the brook in the way." But they drag Him up again, and hurry Him on to the city. They take Him first to the house of Annas, that greedy old Sadducee, who probably had much to do with the part Judas played in the tragedy. Meanwhile the Sanhedrim is being assembled in the house of Caiaphas. Thither they hurry Him, and there the jailer, a poor hireling of the high priest, strikes Him in the face. What hours of suffering He endures here as they wait for daybreak, the mob meanwhile amusing themselves by mocking Him and spitting upon Him.

When the dawn has come the ecclesiastical trial, a mere fiasco, has ended; and then begins the civil trial before Pilate, who happens to be in Jerusalem. After that strange private interview Pilate pronounces Him innocent. But this only adds to the fury of the mob. Then a bright thought strikes Pilate. He will send Him to Herod of Galilee, for Jesus is a Galilean. But the Christ will not speak to this characterless murderer of John the Baptist, and Herod in anger throws a scarlet robe about the prisoner and sends Him back to Pilate. Then Pilate would try to save Him by putting Him side by side with Barabbas, the thug and murderer, and saying, "Which will I release?" And they cry, "Barabbas!" "But what shall I do with Jesus?" And they cry, "Crucify Him! Crucify Him!"

Then Pilate, after washing his hands and declaring himself innocent, orders Him scourged. He is turned over to the cruel Roman soldiers, to whom He is nothing more than "a hunted animal for the dogs to worry." Here He suffers the vilest indignities. Here they make a wreath of thorns and put it on His brow. They have heard that He called Himself a king, and so they put a reed in His hand, and, bowing before Him, mock Him. Here all the baser passions of these Roman butchers are turned loose, and hell itself spits its venom on the Son of God.

Now begins the march to Calvary. He faints beneath the heavy cross they put on His shoulders, but they hurry Him on. Now the hill is reached. With rough hands they strip His garments and bind Him to the cross. They drive the nails through His quivering flesh, and lift up the cross before the eyes of the bloodthirsty multitude. And there He hangs—your dying Lord!

Hear Him cry, "My God, My God, why hast Thou forsaken Me?" Then the darkness thickens. The sun hides its face. A strange silence falls upon the jesting murderers. The mistiness of death gathers on the Saviour's eyes as He cries, "It is finished!" From the city yonder is heard the murmur of voices, and the sound of trumpets, and in the gathering gloom may be seen the column of smoke rising from the altar of burnt sacrifice. But, oh, Jerusalem! the hour of thy desolation has come. What avails your sacrifices now? The glory has departed. Behold the veil is rent in twain, the earth quakes, the rocks are rent, the tombs are opened! Yonder is the sacrifice of heaven—the true Lamb of

God. A cruel world has rejected Him. They have slain their Messiah and King. He is the last and only sacrifice for sin. And that blood-stained cross with its bleeding victim shall yet be the glory of the eternities, and uncounted millions shall turn their eyes of faith towards Golgotha's hill, and through the centuries cry

> Jesus, Thy blood and righteousness
> My beauty are, my glorious dress;
> 'Midst flaming worlds, in these arrayed,
> With joy shall I lift up my head.

Hail! Thou suffering Christ! All hail! Hail! Thou conquering Christ! All hail! The darkness of Calvary is past, and the world is rejoicing in Thy resurrection power and victory. But far be it from me to glory save in Thy cross!

A Prayer

> O Sacred Head, now wounded,
>   With grief and shame weighed down,
> Now scornfully surrounded
>   With thorns, Thine only crown;
> O Sacred Head, what glory,
>   What bliss, till now was Thine!
> Yet, though despised and gory,
>   I joy to call Thee mine.
>
> What language shall I borrow
>   To thank Thee, dearest Friend,
> For this, Thy dying sorrow,
>   Thy pity without end?
> Oh, make me Thine forever;
>   And should I fainting be,
> Lord, let me never, never,
>   Outlive my love to Thee.
>
> Be near me when I'm dying,
>   Oh, show Thy cross to me;
> And, for my succour flying,

Come, Lord, and set me free;
These eyes, new faith receiving,
From Jesus shall not move;
For he who dies believing,
Dies safely, through Thy love.
—*Bernard of Clairvaux.*

VII.

MEDITATION AND THE BIBLE

> But his delight is in the law of the Lord, and in His law doth he meditate day and night.
>
> —*David.*

"THE reason we come away so cold from reading the Word is because we do not warm ourselves at the fire of meditation," said Richard Watson. The Bible is preëminently a book for meditation. It can never be rightly understood and appreciated until we learn to meditate on its great truths. The doors that guard its most precious gems will forever remain bolted to all but meditative souls. The man who has come to delight in the law of the Lord is the man who has learned the blessed secret of meditating day and night on its words. Some people find much of the Bible uninteresting and unprofitable because they have never discovered the way of prayerful meditation. They *skim* the Scriptures rather than *search* the Scriptures. An old writer puts it thus:

"Amongst the insects which subsist on the sweet sap of flowers, there are two very different classes. One is remarkable for its imposing plumage, which shows in the sunlight like the dust of gems; and as you watch its jaunty gyrations over the fields, and its minuet dance from flower to flower, you cannot help admiring its graceful activity, for it is plainly getting over a great deal of ground. But in the same field there is another worker, whose brown vest and businesslike, straightforward flight may not have arrested your eye. His fluttering neighbour darts down here and there, and sips elegantly wherever he can find a drop of ready nectar; but this dingy plodder makes a point of alighting everywhere, and wherever he alights he either finds honey or makes it. If the flower cup be deep, he goes down to the bottom; if its dragon mouth be shut, he thrusts its lips asunder; and if the nectar be peculiar or recondite, he explores all about till he discovers it, and then having ascertained the knack of it, joyful as one who has found great spoil, he sings his way down into its luscious recesses. His rival, of the painted velvet wing, has no patience for such dull and long-winded details. But what is the end? Why, the one died last October along with the flowers; the other is warm in his hive to-night, amidst the fragrant stores which he gathered beneath the bright beams of summer."

It was Leigh Richmond who describes so beautifully one of his visits to the Young Cottager. He found her asleep with her finger on the open Bible before her. She was pointing at the words, "Lord, remember me when Thou comest into Thy kingdom." "Is this casual or designed? thought I. Either way it is remarkable. But in another moment I discovered that her finger was indeed an index to the thoughts of her heart. She half awoke from her dozing state, but not sufficiently so to perceive that any person was present, and said in a kind of whisper, 'Lord, remember me—remember me—remember—remember a poor child; Lord, remember me." That is true meditation, when we appropriate the Word to our own soul need, and make its promises a part of the very life.

One of the great spiritual masters of the last century, Dean Goulburn, formulated some rules for Bible study that should be helpful to every sincere student of the Word. "Meditation on Scripture," said he, "need not be limited to set times, but may be carried on profitably in any hour of solitude, and whenever the mind is not otherwise engaged. Possibly at some interval during the day you may be alone. Have recourse then to the passage of Scripture which you have previously lodged in your mind, and ask yourself seriously, as in the sight of God, what practical lessons it is designed to teach, and what bearing it has on your spiritual welfare. . . . During a solitary walk, or at any period of leisure, imagine that, when you return, you will be called upon to address an audience on the subject which you propose for meditation. It wonderfully disentangles all difficulties to consider how we could, make plain to other minds the truth which is thus beset to our own.

"1. Endeavour to realize the presence of God according to that conception of this great truth which best suits your own mind. Feel that He is here.

"2. Call upon God as an essential condition of success, to inspire you with holy thoughts, and to bless them to your spiritual profit and growth in grace for Christ's sake. Do it very briefly but with great earnestness.

"3. Open the passage of Scripture which is to form the subject of meditation; or repeat it mentally.

"4. The Bible being opened at the passage, picture to yourself the circumstances by an effort of the imagination.

"5. The circumstances having been pictured, next comes the exercise of the understanding upon the words. We reflect upon them, turn them over in our mind, endeavour to make out what they teach, what doctrine is wrapped up in them, and what duty.

"6. Next follows the exercise of the affections and the will, incomparably the most important part of the whole meditation. In this consists the practical application of the little sermon to your own heart, in the absence of which it is useless, or in some respects worse than useless. It will be a good plan to allow any feeling which stirs within you, as you regard the truths of the passage, to express itself in prayer. Conclude all by an exercise of the will, that is, by one or more resolutions."

But to these very helpful rules may be added some other practical suggestions:

1. *Memorize the Scripture.* It is a good plan to commit at least one verse to memory every day. Let this be done upon rising in the morning, then all through the day let that verse be carried in the memory, and from it will flow an ever-freshening stream of comfort and strength and hope. In after life this memorized Scripture will give forth a fragrance that will enrich and beautify life's closing years. For God's children who toil in the fields, or in the factory, or in the office, or in the mine, and who do not have much time to devote to systematic Bible study, this is a good plan. One verse kept in the memory throughout the day may be turned over and over again in the mind until every word flashes with some beautiful lesson.

2. *Read and reread the great passages of the Word.* There is a wonderful variety in the Bible. There is variety of literary structure and style, variety in the religious point of view of the writers, variety in the individuality of the writers, and variety in the spiritual intensity of different parts. But this variety does not interfere with its real unity. There are parts of Scripture however that will appeal with more interest and power to some minds than to others. Yet there are certain passages and chapters of such outstanding beauty and power that all spiritual minds are naturally attracted to them. In

the Old Testament, for instance, such passages as Genesis i., Deuteronomy xxxii.–xxxiv., The Song of Deborah, The Prayer of Hannah, 2 Samuel xxii., Solomon's Prayer of Dedication, Psalms xix., xxiii., xlviii., lxv., lxxii., lxxxiv. and ciii., and Isaiah xl.–lxvi. will never lose their freshness. In the New Testament The Words of Jesus, and such passages as Romans viii., 1 Corinthians xiii., and St. Paul's letter to the Ephesians, we will want to read again and again.

3. *Always seek the aid of the Holy Spirit.* Someone has said that the Bible without the Holy Spirit is like a sun-dial by moonlight. The Holy Spirit is the great Interpreter of Scripture. When, in the quiet hour, the mind and heart are open to His influence He sheds light divine on the sacred page. He uncovers the hidden things of truth. He makes plain the ways of God. "Howbeit when He, the Spirit of Truth is come, He shall guide you into all truth."

Every hour of meditation therefore should begin with prayer for His presence and His enlightening influence. When He is present there will be no time spent in day dreaming. Mind and heart will be wonderfully quickened, and the deep things of God will be uncovered and appropriated to enrich and glorify the life.

A Prayer

Come Holy Ghost, our hearts inspire,
    Let us Thine influence prove;
Source of the old prophetic fire,
    Fountain of life and love.

Come Holy Ghost, for moved by Thee
    The prophets wrote and spoke;
Unlock the truth, Thyself the key,
    Unseal the sacred book.

Expand Thy wings celestial Dove,
    Brood o'er our nature's night;
On our disordered spirits move,
    And let there now be light.

God, through Himself, we then shall know,
    If Thou within us shine;
And sound, with all Thy saints below,
    The depths of love divine.
                        —Charles Wesley.

VIII.

MEDITATION AND PREACHING

> My heart was hot within me;
> While I was musing the fire kindled:
> Then spake I with my tongue.
>
> —*David.*

IT is said of the great and good McCheyne that on Saturday afternoon he was on his way to visit a dying man when he was met by a friend who asked how he could spare time on Saturday for such a purpose. The preacher replied, "I always like before preaching to take a look over the brink." In the minister's preparation for the pulpit nothing else can take the place of the look into the unseen. No brilliancy of mind or natural fervour, no social gift or popularity can permit the preacher to dispense with spiritual contemplation.

We need a revival of the mystical in the Christian ministry to-day. We have swung altogether too far towards the opposite extreme. And when I say mystical I mean it in the best sense of that very expressive word. Dr. Rufus Jones has given us an excellent definition of genuine mystical religion:

"It is not a thing of ecstatic momentary states, and it is not a blinding of the eyes in the hope of discovering another organ to see with. It is a life of normal, joyous correspondence with the presence of God, who streams into every person whose inner windows are open, and who floods every act and impulse with constructive energy."

We have become so practical and so intellectual in these latter days that we seem almost tempted to get along without God. We seem to have lost our consciousness of the unseen and eternal, and thus have lost spiritual depth. Said the Archbishop of Canterbury, "We have high churchmen, and low churchmen, and broad churchmen; what we need is *deep churchmen.*"

For the successful minister spiritual meditation is necessary.

1. *In order to settled conviction concerning the great truths of God.* How can any man preach the great doctrines of the Bible with power unless he have a profound conviction of their truth? He must feel that these great teachings have become a part of his very life. It was Johann Gottlieb Fichte, the prophet of transcendental idealism, and a man of stainless character who said, "*I am a priest of truth*. My life, my fortunes are of little moment—the results of my life are of infinite moment. I have bound myself to venture all things, to suffer all things for truth." And this must be the gospel preacher's ideal concerning his holy vocation. He is a *priest of truth* in the highest sense.

Neglect of spiritual meditation will always be noticeable in the minister. His grasp of truth will be uncertain, and his preaching will produce uncertainty and vacillation in his hearers. There will be little soul food in what he says. Some modern preaching is much like the dish of which Abraham Lincoln speaks as "homeopathic soup made from the shadow of a chicken." It lacks food elements. It does not satisfy spiritual hunger. Prayerful meditation upon the great themes of the Word of God will deepen and fasten the hold of truth on the mind and heart, and produce in the preacher's life such earnestness of conviction concerning the Scriptures that he will not question their inspiration. Then his message will have authority. It will be "in demonstration of the spirit and of power." It will be a message from God, and the people will know that it is.

If the truth were known it would easily be seen that many ministers who are preaching what is called "liberalism" and "new theology" to-day are men who neglected to keep in touch with God through meditation and private devotion. An eminent professor in one of our theological schools says that when he finds a young minister who has fallen into doubt, investigation always reveals the fact that the young man neglected secret prayer and meditation on the great truths of the Bible. Nothing will so quickly take the keen edge off a man's own religious experience, and undermine his faith in the inerrancy of holy Scripture like neglect of spiritual meditation.

2. *In order to patience concerning the visible results of our work.* When we look from a mere human standpoint we shall find plenty of opportunity for discouragement in pastoral and pulpit work. To some of us it is given only to sow without ever seeing the harvest in this life. What need of patience and

complete submission to the will of God! Listen to Milton who, when stricken with blindness and poverty, wrote:

> When I consider how my light is spent,
> Ere half my days, in this dark world and wide,
> And that one talent, which is death to hide,
> Lodged with me useless, though my soul more bent
> To serve therewith my Maker, and present
> My true account, lest He, returning, chide;
> "Doth God exact day-labour, light denied?"
> I fondly ask: but Patience, to prevent
> That murmur, soon replies, "God doth not need
> Either man's work, or His own gifts; who best
> Bear His mild yoke, they serve Him best; His state
> Is kingly: thousands at His bidding speed,
> And post o'er land and water without rest;
> They also serve who only stand and wait."

He who is much in the secret place of communion and meditation will develop the grace of patience and hopefulness, and if faithfully doing his duty as heaven's ambassador will be content to leave results with God.

3. *In order to preparation for the delivery of the message.* A great naturalist of the eighteenth century has suggested one of the secrets of powerful and successful preaching. He says: "Invention depends on patience. Contemplate your subject long; it will gradually unfold, till a sort of electric spark convulses for a moment the brain, and spreads down to the very heart a glow of irritation. Then come the luxuries of genius, the true hours for production and composition; hours so delightful that I have spent twelve and fourteen successively at my writing desk and have still been in a state of pleasure." The mental preparation is always necessary. The thought must take fire before the words take fire. But if there be mental preparation only, the message will not be what it should be. We must come from a vision of the heavenly if we would be true messengers of God.

We are threatened to-day with a spirit of professionalism in the pulpit; and apostolic ideals have been all but lost sight of by many who assume the sacred office of the Christian ministry. It was the great Apostle to the Gentiles who said, "But far be it from me to glory, save in the cross of our Lord Jesus Christ, through which the world hath been crucified unto me, and I unto the world." He who would maintain an ideal like this must be much alone with God. He must see something of the relative value of the earthly and the heavenly, and he must see something of the real glory of the cross of Christ. When he has meditated on the sacrificial death of his Lord until his heart is aflame with love then his words will be as fire whenever and wherever he speaks.

That is a beautiful legend of the Feast of St. Francis of Assisi and St. Clara in the Church of St. Mary and the Angels. "And at the first dish," runs the legend, "St. Francis began to speak of God so sweetly, so sublimely, so wondrously, that the fullness of divine grace came down on them, and they were rapt in God. And as they were thus rapt, with eyes and hands uplift to heaven, the folk of Assisi and the country round about saw that St. Mary and the Angels, and all the house, and the wood that was hard by the house, were burning brightly, and it seemed as if it were a great fire that filled the church and the house and the whole wood together. For which cause the people of Assisi ran thither in great haste to quench the flames—but coming close up to the house, and finding no fire at all, they entered within and found St. Francis and St. Clara and all their company in contemplation rapt in God and sitting around that humble board. Whereby of a truth they understood that this had been a heavenly flame, and no earthly one at all."

Neglect of meditation upon the great verities of Scripture will mean a shallow intellectualism or a lazy formalism for the preacher. There will be no blood-red earnestness in his manner; there will be no flame in his words. He will have no heart grip on his congregation because he has not waited in meditation and prayer until the truth he preaches has gripped his own soul.

4. *In order to a right conception of the glory of his high calling.* What a high ideal the Apostle Paul had for the calling and work of the ministry! He speaks of "the mystery of the Gospel for which I am an ambassador in chains." He exhorts Timothy to be a "good minister of Jesus Christ, nourished in the words of the faith," and charges him "in the sight of God, who quickeneth all things, and of Christ Jesus, who before Pontius Pilate witnessed the good confession; that thou keep the commandment, without spot, without reproach, until the appearing of our Lord Jesus Christ."

"Suffer hardships," he says again, "with me, as a good soldier of Christ Jesus," and "preach the word; be instant in season, out of season; reprove, rebuke, exhort, with all long-suffering and teaching." Is it likely that we ever would have had such words as these had not Paul been turned aside from his ceaseless travels into a Roman dungeon? There he had time to pen these immortal letters that have in them such richness of thought and experience, and that bear so plainly the marks of the hours spent in holy meditation.

Through the multiplicity of organizations and departments in modern church work it is to be feared that the pulpit is fast becoming secularized. In some communities the minister is no longer a preacher. He is the business manager for the various departments of church activity. In other communities he is the ecclesiastical administrator, or the social leader. There is a constant temptation in these days for the minister to "forsake the Word of God and serve tables." In many churches a man is valued more for his administrative ability than for his power to preach the Gospel or teach the Word of God. Such a man must find the secret place, and meditate on those things that led him to enter this holy office, and then ask himself whether he is really doing the work to which the Holy Spirit called him.

The minister who finds time for contemplation of the great verities and awful sublimities of time and eternity, as set forth in the Scriptures, will quickly come to a high conception of his mission as an ambassador of the King of kings. He will see that his great work is *to preach the Gospel*. Such a man will have no time for mere intellectual gymnastics in the pulpit. He will seek to be a great preacher, but a great preacher after the apostolic ideal. And the consciousness of the greatness of his calling will give to his messages a tone of heavenly authority that has been made sweet and tender by hours of waiting in the inner chamber with his Lord.

5. *In order to be saved from the sin of living a selfish life.* The conditions of modern church life are often such as to expose the minister to this subtle temptation. The tendency towards professionalism makes it easy for the man who is much before the public to drift into self-living. To be sure only the grace of God can cleanse us from selfishness, but we must be conscious of our need, we must see ourselves as God sees us before we will seek this cleansing. What a beautiful example of the unselfish spirit we have in Barnabas. He had been sent as a delegate from the church at Jerusalem to the church at Antioch. But he soon decided that Paul was the man for the situation there, and accordingly went to Tarsus and found Paul and brought him to Antioch. He

was more anxious for the success of the church at Antioch and for the coming of the kingdom of Christ than for his own position or popularity; so he surrendered the leadership to another whom he believed to be better fitted for the place. What a beautiful spirit of magnanimity! How much we need it in the Christian ministry to-day! If we could have more time to meditate on the unselfishness of Christ we would oftener "show forth the Gospel of the Son of God," and would be more effective in the "greatest work in the world." A few words left us by St. Francis reveal the secret of his marvellous influence, and might well be pondered by us upon whom is the call of heaven to preach the everlasting Gospel:

"Above all the gifts and the graces which the Holy Spirit gives to His friends is the grace to conquer oneself, and willingly to suffer pain, outrages, disgrace, and evil treatment for the love of Christ."

A Prayer

Oh, Lord, save me from praying with a cold heart, and from witnessing for Thee in cold blood! I am the child of Thy covenant, I am the ransomed of the Lord, I am the purchase of Calvary; and shall I live with a cold heart, and speak with a cold heart, and witness with careless words? Send me, oh, Lord, to the inner chamber of meditation where Thy Spirit can warm my heart and teach me the way of true prayer. Help me to live the sacrificial life, and so "fill up that which is behind of the afflictions of Christ." My prayer too often has been so cold and heartless, and my life so selfish, and my words so professional that I have shamed Thee again and again. In bitterness of soul do I repent of my sin and plead for Thy mercy. Show me Thy favour, oh, God, and teach me the way of holy fellowship and soul intercession.

IX.

MEDITATION AND WORSHIP

> Within my heart is the Eternal Adoration.
> —*Tersteegen.*

EVERY age has its own peculiar needs, and these are always apparent when conditions are carefully studied. The day of Francis of Assisi was characterized by papal absolutism and dense superstition, and the great need of that time was an inspiration that would result in intellectual quickening and independence of thought. The age that preceded the time of the Wesleys was one of intellectual doubt and spiritual deadness. It preceded the birth of industrialism and a new political and social consciousness. Had not the Wesleyan revival come England would doubtless have been plunged into a civil maelstrom similar to that of the French Revolution. An eminent student of history declares that Wesley did more to save England than Chatham.

This age has its peculiar needs. Dr. Adam Smith says: "Ours is an age so charged with the instinct of work, so empty of God, of reverence and of prayer." The tendency has been towards the grossest materialism resulting in an indifference to the great problems of life and destiny. Dr. Campbell Morgan recently said that the attitude of the world today could be summed up in one word, "indifference." Because of this spirit of indifference the supernatural has become a bugbear to many. Criticism of the Word of God and the Church has been rampant. Many have the form of godliness without the power. We need a new spiritual consciousness—a new touch of the Divine—a God consciousness. Only this can stay the flood-tide of scepticism and materialism and irreverence already all about us.

See how little of the spirit of true worship there is in many churches. It would seem as if the desire for musical entertainment, or for intellectual gymnastics had almost entirely superseded the desire for real spiritual worship. Suppose that in the average congregation the question, "Why are you at church?" were asked each person, and each should answer honestly, what would be the result? Some, doubtless, would be there to hear a good sermon, others to hear the music, others from a sense of duty, others to meet friends, and yet others from habit. But how few might be found there because of a sincere desire to worship God. Is not this the reason why there is so little of the presence and power of the Holy Spirit in many of our church services? And may not this condition be traced directly to the fact that we give so little thought to, and make so little preparation for, the hour of worship? Do we go to church to meet God? Do we expect to hear His message? Have we given time to heart preparation for the reception of God's message? How different would be the spirit in which many of us enter the place of holy worship if we really expected to be face to face with our Lord! An incident in the life of the late Dr. A. J. Gordon of the Clarendon Street Baptist Church, Boston, transformed his ministry and made his church a great centre of spiritual power. It can be told best in Dr. Gordon's own words:

"It was Saturday night, when wearied with the work of preparing Sunday's sermon, that I fell asleep and the dream came. I was in the pulpit before a full congregation, just ready to begin my sermon, when a stranger entered and passed slowly up the left aisle of the church looking first to the one side and then to the other as though silently asking with his eyes that someone would give him a seat. He had proceeded nearly half-way up the aisle when a gentleman stepped out and offered him a place in his pew, which was quietly accepted. Excepting the face and features of the stranger everything in the scene is distinctly remembered—the number of the pew, the Christian man who offered its hospitality, the exact seat which was occupied. Only the countenance of the visitor could never be recalled. That his face wore a peculiarly serious look, as of one who had known some great sorrow, is clearly impressed on my mind. His bearing too was exceeding humble, his dress poor and plain, and from the beginning to the end of the service he gave the most respectful attention to the preacher. Immediately as I began my sermon my attention became riveted on this hearer. If I would avert my eyes from him for a moment they would instinctively return to him, so that he held my attention rather than I held his till the discourse was ended.

"To myself I said constantly, 'Who can that stranger be?' and then I mentally resolved to find out by going to him and making his acquaintance as soon as the service should be over. But after the benediction had been given the departing congregation filled into the aisles and before I could reach him the visitor had left the house. The gentleman with whom he had sat remained behind, however and approaching him with great eagerness I asked: 'Can you tell me who that stranger was who sat in your pew this morning?' In the most matter-of-course way he replied: 'Why, do you not know that man? It was Jesus of Nazareth.' With a sense of the keenest disappointment I said: 'My dear sir, why did you let Him go without introducing me to Him? I was so desirous to speak with Him.' And with the same nonchalant air the gentleman replied: 'Oh, do not be troubled. He has been here to-day, and no doubt He will come again.'"

Jesus of Nazareth is present in every place where His people are gathered for worship. "Lo, I am with you alway." But do we expect to meet Him? And do we always recognize Him? Is not this one of the most cruel sins of the age—our failure to recognize the Lord in His Holy Place? And is not this failure often the direct result of so little meditation preceding the hour of worship?

There are three things peculiar to this age that supplant meditation, and thus hinder the preparation for holy worship.

1. *Non-religious reading.* The Sunday morning newspaper has become an enormous factors in the life of the American people, and is one of the greatest hindrances to holy worship that can be named. Its pages are often reeking with every form of social corruption and nonsense, easily destroying the soul's appetite for spiritual food. The man who spends his Sunday mornings wallowing in the filth of the criminal, social, and sporting columns of the average Sunday newspaper will have no time or disposition to prepare himself by meditation for the hour of worship. And if he does attend the house of God he will likely have little appreciation of that which is spiritual and soul strengthening in the service.

In the cheap story magazine may be found, too, the husks upon which many young people are feeding their minds during the hours of the Lord's day. The vicious suggestions and inane plots and stories to be found in much of the cheap magazine literature that is being sown broadcast over the land is anything but helpful to thoughtfulness and prayer. Parents who allow their children to feed on this kind of mental food will almost surely find them growing up with little desire for the place of worship and little appreciation of the spiritual life.

2. *Criticism of the ministry and the message.* In too many homes to-day parents fall into the habit of criticizing the preacher and the sermon. On the way from the place of worship and around the dinner table children and young people sometimes hear unkind references to the sermon and to the messenger of heaven. We forget that God is jealous for the men whom He calls and anoints to be His ambassadors and bear His message to a lost world. Once upon a time when a woman criticized God's servant, Moses, she was stricken with the deadly leprosy, and the story of Miriam has stood through the ages as a warning to all who would touch God's anointed or do His prophets harm. There is no surer way of destroying the influence of the gospel message than by this method of criticism, and there is no surer way of making certain that little time will be spent in preparation for the hour of worship. Let the atmosphere of unkind criticism of ministers and churches pervade the home circle, then children and young people will soon lose their respect for the house of God, and there will be no disposition to spend the hours of the Sabbath morning in thinking and reading upon sacred themes. Only he who reverences the house of God and respects the Christian ministry will have time for meditation and prayer in preparation for public worship.

3. *The insatiable desire for riches.* This is fast becoming the national sin, and more, perhaps, than any one thing that can be mentioned is responsible for the small church attendance in many communities, and for the little interest shown by many professing Christians in the services of the sanctuary. When the people of any nation set themselves to seek the things of this world they soon lose interest in Christ and in the coming of His kingdom. Among the best things that Ian Maclaren ever said were these words: "About one thing only we ought to be anxious, and that is the relation between the people and Christ. If they should cease to believe in Christ, their homes and gardens and schools and plenty would avail them little, for the kingdom of the people would only end in a secular paradise, and the soul of the nation would die. It were better for the nation to be ill-fed and ill-clothed, better to have no share in government, and only the poorest means of education, than to lose the inspiration of faith, and the hope of a world to come. What lends glory to this earth is the arch of heaven above us, and the sun which gives its colour to the tiniest flower; and what lends dignity to life is the sense of eternity, and the fellowship of man with God."

Our Lord and Master knew well the result of setting the heart upon earthly things, and declared that it was easier for a camel to go through the eye of a needle than for a man who sets his heart upon riches to enter the kingdom of heaven. He whose idol is riches is more likely to have his mind upon his business plans on the morning of the Lord's Day than upon the things that fit the mind and heart for holy worship. Meditation upon sacred things will have little place in the life of the worldling.

How blessed to come to the sanctuary with the heart and mind prepared for communion with the Highest! Then every song will be an act of worship, and every prayer will throb with life, and every sermon will be to us the message of God. Then every place of worship will be a place where we meet God face to face, and the humblest church edifice will contain the Shekinah of heaven. Then Bishop Bickersteth's lovely hymn will have a new meaning for us:

A Hymn

>Come ye yourselves apart and rest a while,
>   Weary, I know it of the press and throng,
>Wipe from your brow the sweat and dust of toil,
>   And in My quiet strength again be strong.
>
>Come ye aside from all the world holds dear,
>   For converse which the world has never known,
>Alone with Me, and with My Father here,
>   With Me and with My Father not alone.
>
>Come, tell me all that ye have said and done,
>   Your victories and failures, hopes and fears.
>I know how hardly souls are wooed and won:
>   My choicest wreaths are always wet with tears,
>
>Come ye and rest: the journey is too great,
>   And ye will faint beside the way and sink:
>The bread of life is here for you to eat,
>   And here for you the wine of love to drink.

Then fresh from converse with your Lord return,
    And work till daylight softens into even:
The brief hours are not lost in which ye learn
    More of your Master and His rest in heaven.

X.

MEDITATION AND RESERVE POWER

> In quietness and in confidence shall be your strength.
> —*Isaiah.*

ENTHUSIASM is one thing; mere noise quite another. Real enthusiasm is the fruitage of strength of life; mere noise may be an indication of weakness. John Wesley was wise enough to distinguish between the two, and exhorted his preachers to beware of screaming. Wesley knew very well that the secret of power was in that holy waiting before God which begets strength through confidence.

Now there can be no real enthusiasm in life where there is not always a good supply reserve power. So many live "from hand to mouth" in mental and spiritual things. This was surely not the plan of our Heavenly Father. See with what prodigality He has endowed this physical body of ours. It is a well-known fact, for instance, that the bones of the human body have a much greater resisting power than is needed under ordinary circumstances, and that while we have two lungs we can get along very comfortably with one, or if we lose five-sixths of the thyroid gland we can, get along very nicely with what remains. And is there not here a suggestion that He who created the human body has provided just as lavish mental and spiritual equipment, and that these reserve possibilities should be nourished and developed just as carefully as our physical powers?

The man who gives attention to the development of his reserves will have, a great advantage in life both from the standpoint of efficiency and enjoyment. Sir Joshua Reynolds said, "A picture must not only be done well, but it must seem to have been done easily." To have power with men we must give the impression of sufficiency, and we cannot give this impression unless we have the reality. And the reality can only be found by the development of our reserve powers through meditation and study and prayer.

The temptation of modern life is to pay little attention to this matter, but to use up all the power we have in the daily rush of business or pleasure. "America's greatest need," said a certain European writer, "is repose, time to stop and take breath." Unless the people of this nation pause in their mad hurry towards wealth and social enjoyment, and give more attention to the development of the inner life the fountains of national vigour and success will soon run dry.

New reserve power means courage. There never was a day in the history of the race when men have needed more than now a militant courage. There is in this day a dearth of great spiritual leaders—men who will dare to stand for the right, and whom God can trust in the crisis. Moses developed reserve power in the wilds of Horeb, and he became mighty in leadership and courageous in the face of great difficulties. David developed reserve power watching the flocks in the quiet of Judea's hills, and his name shall endure while the world lasts. And looking at our Lord and Master from the standpoint of His human nature shall we not say that during these years of quiet in Nazareth, while He "advanced in wisdom and stature and in favour with God and men," He was laying up a supply of reserve force that should carry Him through the hardships and struggles of His active earthly ministry? In the face of the severest temptations, and in the face of desertion and betrayal by friends His courage never failed. And there is a great call to-day for men of unwavering courage who will take their stand in every realm of human activity and scorn to compromise with wrong, men of high moral conviction and kingliness of soul whose courage will not falter. Such men must come from the secret place of communion and meditation where exhaustless supplies of reserve power have been generated and stored in the life.

If we would develop reserve power we must first be cleansed from the defilement of sin. Sin weakens and paralyzes from every high purpose and every noble ambition. When foul thoughts fill the heart and evil passions sway the life there can be no true development of life's reserves. We must be able to say sincerely

"Make my breast
Transparent as pure crystal, that the world,
Jealous of me, may see the foulest thought
My heart does hold."

To be a reservoir of power the life must be cleansed from that which destroys power. Just so long as an unconfessed and unforgiven sin remains in the heart there can be no consciousness of spiritual power. In the quiet hour the Spirit of God will uncover every hidden sin, and every secret thought, and show us our need for cleansing. The earnest soul will always welcome such light and fly at once to Him whose blood "cleanseth from all sin."

To develop reserve power we must have a definite purpose in life. The shilly-shally, pleasure-loving, amusement-seeking existence with which some people seem content will never develop any reserve force. How few young people in these days have any high aim in life. Go into any high school or college and call for those who have definitely decided upon some great life purpose, and see how few will respond. The majority of young people in the average community are like driftwood in the river's current. They have really given little thought to the matter of definiteness of aim in life. And from this class, in future years, shall come the men and women who will fill our jails and penitentiaries and pauper houses and lunatic asylums. They allow themselves to drift until life loses its halo and there is nothing but the black stormy sea of remorse and despair before them. Pitiable indeed is the condition of the life that has been lived with no high purpose, and terrible the ruin that often follows.

The man without a purpose is the man only partly alive. There are heaven-born gifts and faculties in his nature of which he has never been conscious and which are dying through neglect. Somebody once painted a picture of the resurrection in which he tried to represent the work as only half done. Of course it was a freak picture. Some were alive to their waists, some had one arm alive, some were represented with half of the head alive. But that picture is quite possible in human life. There are many who for want of a high purpose are only partly alive. They have not given time to thought concerning any great work, and have no consciousness of the sublime possibilities wrapped up in their lives.

To develop reserve power we must often be quiet. How richly expressive of soul quiet is that second verse of the twenty-third psalm: "He maketh me to lie down in green pastures; He leadeth me beside the still waters. He restoreth my soul." The distraction and worry of this strenuous age kill more people than any disease that can be named. Some very eminent medical men declare that the alarming increase in insanity in recent years may be traced directly to the strenuousness of modern life. Moments of quiet thought refresh and renew mind and heart. An hour of meditation in the presence chamber of God will always restore soul poise and give new strength. The crowded, feverish days of business and social activity quickly use up the soul's vital forces, but the season of quiet thought and communion with heaven not only quickly restores spiritual vitality but enables us to lay up a reserve supply against the days to come.

Finally, to develop reserve power we must think much on the power and boundless grace of God. "In Him we live and move and have our being." Jesus said, "All authority hath been given unto Me in heaven and on earth. Go ye therefore...." He said too, "If ye abide in Me and My words abide in you, ask whatsoever ye will and it shall be done unto you." He who is the source of all power and authority has promised to bestow all needed power and grace upon us. "Ye shall receive power when the Holy Spirit is come upon you." Paul became a partaker of this divine power and he exclaimed, "I can do all things in Him that strengtheneth me." When our thought dwells on the boundless power and mercy of God faith will be strengthened to appropriate power. We shall not only see our barrenness and need, but we shall see our high privilege in Christ and shall seek the infilling of the Holy Spirit, God's promised Gift. And he who has received the Holy Spirit has found a never failing source of strength and grace and wisdom.

A Prayer

Dear Lord and Father of Mankind,
    Forgive our feverish ways!
Re-clothe us in our rightful mind;
In purer lives Thy service find,
    In deeper reverence, praise.

Drop Thy still dews of quietness,
    Till all our strivings cease;
Take from our souls the strain and stress,
And let our ordered lives confess
    The beauty of Thy peace.

Breathe through the heats of our desire
    Thy coolness and Thy balm;
Let sense be dumb, let flesh retire:
Speak through the earthquake, wind, and fire,
    Oh, still small voice of calm!
—John G. Whittier.

XI.

MEDITATION AND SOUL WINNING

> Now then we are ambassadors for Christ, as though God did beseech you by us: we pray you in Christ's stead, be ye reconciled to God.
>
> —*Paul.*

IT was George Whitfield who said, "When I wake I am planning to save souls. When I sleep I am dreaming of saving souls and my whole heart's desire is to save souls." The true Christian's great business is to save souls. Whether he be in the pulpit or in the pew he should be a soul winner. Of course it is the gospel minister's great business. Professor Phelps used to say that the man who had lost interest in men was fit only for a seminary. Somebody has suggested that he might have said with perhaps more truth, "is fit only for a cemetery." But our Lord did not intend that the work of soul saving should be confined to the ministry. He insisted that every Christian should be His witness. "Ye shall be witnesses unto Me" He said to the early Church; and if there had been found in the early Church a man or woman who was not doing something to win others to Christ the sincerity of that Christian's experience would have been seriously doubted.

But the best way to learn the art of soul winning is not from books on soul winning, nor from lectures on that subject, although these may be very helpful. Isaac Walton has a suggestion that is applicable here. He says:

"Now for the art of catching fish, that is to say, how to make a man—that was not—to be an angler by a book; he that undertakes it shall undertake a harder task than Mr. Hales, a most valiant and excellent fencer, who in the printed book called 'A Private School of Defense' undertook to teach that art or science, and was laughed at for his labour—not that many useful things might be learned by that book, but he was laughed at because that art was not to be taught by words."

And you cannot learn soul winning by words. One may get many helpful suggestions from books and lectures, but until a man has trodden the quiet way of meditation he can never be a very successful soul winner. In the quiet of that way he must let the Holy Spirit be his teacher.

We must meditate upon the authority of our commission. The King of kings has sent us, and He has said, "He that receiveth you receiveth Me." When we invite men and women to be reconciled to God we do it in the name of Christ and as His ambassadors, and this is true of all Christian workers whether they be ministers or laymen. How this note of divine authority would transform much modern preaching. How little of the consciousness of heavenly ambassadorship there is in some pulpits. Shortly before his death, Joseph Parker, the great London preacher, said: "We have lost the *royal element* in our preaching; we are now making apologies, we are now asking permissions, we are now requesting to be allowed that Christ should be heard along with teachers venerable by their antiquity and dignified by the general pureness of their tone. The preacher now has no kingdom to set up, but some little apology to offer. Now the cry is not 'Lift up your heads, oh, ye gates, and be ye lift up, ye everlasting doors, and the king of glory shall come in,'—it is some weaker cry, some paltry tone of excuse, or some dainty endeavour to escape the tragedy of the occasion. Christianity is nothing if not a kingdom."

In the quiet hour of prayerful waiting before God we are girded with the strength of authority to speak the message of the Highest. Then we shall no more apologize for our mission, but go forth with the consciousness that we are heralds of the King of Glory.

We must meditate upon the worth of a soul until we come to see something of its infinite value. The materialistic drift of modern life has lessened the emphasis upon the value of the soul. The tendency has been to emphasize the things of time and sense, and preach what is called the "gospel of success" instead of the gospel of salvation by the blood of Christ. And so it has come to pass that some ministers and some Sunday-school workers seem to think it more important to be known as interesting and entertaining speakers than to be known as soul winners.

When we lose sight of the immortality of man, and lose faith in the supernatural in religion, then the soul will have lost much of its worth. But when our thought dwells on the soul's eternal destiny, and we meditate on what God has done for the soul's redemption, then we shall easily come to see that there is "nothing really great on earth but man, and nothing really great in man but his soul."

We must meditate upon the necessity for a holy life if we would be soul winners. The matter of character is of first importance in witnessing for God. When we come to help men and women to Christ it is much more necessary that we should be known to be godly than to be known as great scholars or great theologians. The author of "The Price of Power" has a terse paragraph on this point: "We can never have power until we are implicitly obedient to all that we know of God's will regarding our own personal lives. The direction and force of external aim is always determined by the fashion of inner life, and power is always according to purity. If there is anything known to be unholy, unclean, unworthy, yet willfully persisted in, we shall pray in vain for an enduement with the power of God. The one thing needed on the part of a man who realizes his lack of power is honestly to pray: 'Search me, oh, God,' and to wait in the presence of God that He may do it."

Some years ago a man was sent to India as a missionary. But when he undertook to learn the language he found himself utterly unable to master it. After trying for some time he decided to ask to be returned home. But when the people among whom he had lived heard that he was likely to be recalled they petitioned the missionary society not to remove him, declaring that he was more helpful to them than any other missionary. For while he could not speak their language his life was such as to have a mighty influence for good over all the people of the community. He was permitted to remain, and lived and died among them.

Unless we keep before us constantly, and meditate much on the highest New Testament standard of Christian living, we shall be likely to lose the keen edge from our Christian experience and come to have fanatical notions concerning what constitutes a holy life. A little girl when asked the question in her Sunday-school class, "What is holiness?" replied, "Holiness is the way our pastor lives." *Holiness is Christ seen in us*. And lives the probability is that the more Christ is seen in our words and actions the less we will have to say about it ourselves, and the mightier our influence will be to win others to Christ. When Moses came down from the mountain of quiet communion with God he did not need to tell the people that his face shone. And when we spend much time in holy fellowship with heaven the people among whom we move will know that we are heaven's messengers, and there will be such authority and power in our words as will make us successful soul winners.

A Hymn

Jesus, the truth and power divine,
Send forth these messengers of Thine;
Their hands confirm, their hearts inspire,
And touch their lips with hallowed fire.

Be Thou their mouth and wisdom,—Lord;
Thou, by the hammer of Thy word,
The rocky hearts in pieces break,
And bid the suns of thunder speak.

To those who would their Lord embrace,
Give them to preach the word of grace;
Sweetly their yielding bosoms move,
And melt them with the fire of love.

Let all with thankful hearts confess
Thy welcome messengers of peace;
Thy power in their report be found,
And let Thy feet behind them sound.

—Charles Wesley.

XII.

MEDITATION AND VISION

> Having the eyes of your understanding enlightened.
> —*Paul to the Ephesians.*

MEDITATION takes the veil off truth. The highest peaks of truth are never reached either by analysis or synthesis. Only he who has soul vision can see the way to the heights. And it was Plato who taught that the human mind has a native capacity for beatific vision. This is the soul's heritage, God created. Had it not been for sin the soul would have never lost its birthright. But sin has done its deadly work. Spiritual vision has been destroyed in many a life.

None knew better than King Solomon the truth of his own proverb, "Where there is no vision the people cast off restraint." When vision goes, then come rioting and wantonness and all ungodliness. Blindly, men rush to their own destruction. What need then for the restoration of spiritual vision to the race! If every Christian worker could say with the saintly Augustine, "Our whole work is to heal the eye of the heart by which we see God," what a new inspiration would come in all our work.

Now the history of nations is in a very large sense the history of great men. Sometimes it is a William the Conqueror, then a Frederic the Great, then a Napoleon, but the crowning events of national history cluster about great personalities. And what is the history of nations but a record of how God has been lifting the world out of darkness and chaos into light and order by the leadership of great men. There is a special sense in which God has always had His man ready to turn the scale of events and fit them into His eternal purposes. We do not always know about the burning bush, or the Damascus road, or the celestial cross, or the Brescian convent, but God has a program, and there are no breaks in His plan. To His chosen leaders God always vouchsafes a vision, and happy is the man who is "not disobedient to the heavenly vision."

It is said of Moses that "he endured as seeing Him who is invisible." In the lonely mountains of Horeb, keeping watch over his father-in-law's flocks, he had ample time to ponder the great mysteries of life. And what a place for meditation! "Were I a painter," said a certain modern traveller, "and could I illustrate Dante's Inferno, I would have pitched my camp-stool here and have filled my sketch-book, for there could never be wanting to the limner of the dark abyss of the pit, landscapes savage, terribly, unmeasurably sad, unutterably wild, unapproachably grand and awful." Here it was that this man of destiny caught glimpses of the light ineffable, and saw the wild acacia aflame with the fire of God. He had a vision of duty and responsibility to God that transformed his life and made him the messenger and ambassador of heaven. And such a vision must have every true statesman and minister and leader. He may be a politician, but never a statesman until he gets the vision. He may be a deacon, or an elder, or a priest, but never a flaming evangel for Christ until he gets the vision.

Such a vision had Savonarola, the prophet of the renaissance, when yonder in the little Brescian convent he meditated upon the Word of God and practiced the presence of God until his heart was aflame. He went down into the streets of the wicked city of Florence, and preached Christ and Him crucified. Lorenzo himself trembled at the words of this bold young monk who seemed to have no fear of the face of man.

Such a vision, too, had Wendell Phillips, a graduate of Cambridge, who had every prospect for worldly success and greatness. But from his office window he had seen a fellow man kicked through the streets and hurried to the jail by a cruel, bloodthirsty mob. That night this young patrician—lawyer could not sleep. There came before him a vision of a multitude of suffering human beings. Next morning he rose from his bed to dedicate his life to the liberation of the slave. And such a vision must have every great reformer and leader of men.

Now vision *gives freshness and vigour to life.* The life without vision is a life of drudgery and hopelessness. All its work and is commonplace and disappointing. How many there are to-day to whom life seems to have lost its freshness! If they live at all it is in the past. There is no mental or spiritual overflow in life. The vigour and joyousness of earlier days have departed. Life has no bloom. But this should never be true of the child of God. He has a fountain of perpetual youth. At the Feast of Tabernacles Jesus stood and cried saying, "If any man thirst let him come unto Me and drink. He that believeth on Me, as the Scripture hath said, from within him shall flow rivers of living water." The saintly John MacNeil, in his "Spirit Filled Life," speaking of this remarkable Scripture, said: "This promise is for *you*. Has it then been verified in your life and experience? If not, why not? Is there not a cause? But note more closely its hugeness, its godlike vastness. Rivers! not a tricklet or a babbling brook—by its babbling proclaiming its shallowness—or a stream, or a river, but Rivers! What divine prodigality! It is the Brisbane, the Clarence, the Hawkesbury, the Murray, the Murrumbidgee, the Tamar and the Derwent all rolled into one—RIVERS! By the widest, wildest stretch of imagination could it be said of you that 'Rivers of living water' are flowing from you—'flowing,' mind you, 'flowing'? See the freshness, the freedom, and the spontaneity of the service; no force-pump work about the flowing of the rivers; none of the hard labour of the 'soul in prison' (Ps. cxlii. 7). When the rivers begin to flow the worker may sell his force-pump; his prayer has been answered, 'Bring my soul out of prison.'"

"It is worth noting the gradation in John iii., iv., vii. In John iii. 7 we have 'Life' in its beginnings—the new birth. In John iv. 14 we have 'Life abundantly'—'a well of water springing up.' The secret of the perennial upspringing is in the word 'drink-e-t-h'; 'he that drinketh'—not takes a drink, but drinks and drinks and keeps on drinking—that man never thirsts; for how can a man's soul be dry and thirsty with a well of water in it? Many people are living in the third of John,—they have 'Life,' but it is not strong and vigorous; they are suffering from deficient vitality,—when Jesus wants them to be in the fourth enjoying 'Life Abundantly.' The difference in the two experiences is well illustrated in the case of Hagar. In Genesis xxi. 14 we read that Abraham gave Hagar a 'bottle of water' and sent her away. As she wandered in the wilderness 'the water was spent in the bottle' (verse fifteen). But in verse nineteen, 'God opened her eyes, and she saw a well of water.' There are *bottle* Christians, and there are *well* Christians."

Vision *makes us conscious of the nearness of God*. The great need of the age is a new GOD CONSCIOUSNESS. We need a revival of mysticism in its best sense. There is a doctrine taught by the Roman Catholic Church which maintains that the bread and wine of the sacrament become the real flesh and blood of Christ. We need a renewal—not of the doctrine of transubstantiation, but of the doctrine of the *real presence*. Too many live now as if under an empty heaven, forgetting that we are "compassed about with so great a cloud of witnesses," and that "we are made a spectacle unto the world, both to angels and to men." Did not Jesus say, "Lo, I am with you alway"? Did not He say, "If a man love Me, he will keep My word: and My Father will love him, and we will come unto him, and make our abode with him"? If we are His children the Lord proposes to keep us company in every hour of life, but how often we forget this and lose the consciousness of His presence. "He walks as in the presence of God," said good Jeremy Taylor, "that converses with Him in frequent prayer and frequent communion; that runs to Him in all his necessities; that asks counsel of Him in all his doubtings; that opens all his wants to Him; that weeps before Him for his sins that asks remedy and support for his weakness; that fears Him as a judge; reverences Him as a Lord, and obeys Him as a Father." How much brighter and better life would be for many of us if we practiced the presence of God, and lived in the consciousness of His smile.

Vision *gives purity of intention*. Only when we begin to see things as they really are can we be at our best. A wrong estimate of life will always mean a wrong motive; and a wrong motive in life means eternal disaster. It was while reading and meditating upon that immortal passage from "Holy Living and Dying" that John Wesley was led to the supreme surrender of all his powers to God. Let us ponder it here, praying God that as we do so we may have such a vision as will purify every motive of our lives.

"This grace (purity of intention) is so excellent that it sanctifies the most common actions of our life; and yet so necessary that, without it, the very best actions of our devotion are imperfect and vicious. For, as to know the end distinguishes a man from a beast, so to choose a good end distinguishes him from an evil man. The praise is not in the thing done, but in the manner of its doing. If a man visits his sick friend, and watches at his pillow for charity's sake and because of his old affection, we approve it; but if he does it in hope of a legacy he is a vulture, and only watches for the carcass. The same things are honest and dishonest; the manner of doing them, the end of the design, makes the separation.

"Holy intention is to the actions of a man that which the soul is to the body, or form to its matter, or the root to the tree, or the sun to the world, or the fountain to a river, or the base to a pillar; for without these the body is a dead trunk, the matter is sluggish, the tree is a block, the world is darkness, the river is quickly dry, the pillar rushes into flatness and a ruin; and the action is sinful, or unprofitable and vain.

"In every action reflect upon the end and in your undertaking it consider why you do it, and what you propound to yourself for a reward.

"Let every action and concernment be begun with prayer, that God would not only bless the action but sanctify your purpose; and make an oblation of the action to God.

"It is likely our hearts are pure and our intentions spotless when we are not solicitous of the opinion and censures of men, but only that what we do be our duty and accepted of God. For our eyes will certainly be fixed there from whence we expect our reward; and if we desire that God should approve us it is a sign we do His work and expect Him our paymaster.

"He loves virtue for God's sake and its own, that loves and honours it wherever it is to be seen. But he that is envious or angry at a virtue that is not his own, at the perfection or excellency of his neighbour, is not covetous of the virtue, but of its reward and reputation; and then his intentions are polluted. It was a great ingenuity in Moses that wished all the people might be prophets; but if he had designed his own honour he would have prophesied alone. But he that desires only that the work of God and religion him from an evil man. The praise is not in the thing done, but in the manner of its doing. If a man visits his sick friend, and watches at his pillow for charity's sake and because of his old affection, we approve it; but if he does it in hope of a legacy he is a vulture, and only watches for the carcass. The same things are honest and dishonest; the manner of doing them, the end of the design, makes the separation.

"Holy intention is to the actions of a man that which the soul is to the body, or form to its matter, or the root to the tree, or the sun to the world, or the fountain to a river, or the base to a pillar for without these the body is a dead trunk, the matter is sluggish, the tree is a block, the world is darkness, the river is quickly dry, the pillar rushes into flatness and a ruin and the action is sinful, or unprofitable and vain.

"In every action reflect upon the end; and in your undertaking it consider why you do it, and what you propound to yourself for a reward.

"Let every action and concernment be begun with prayer, that God would not only bless the action but sanctify your purpose; and make an oblation of the action to God.

"It is likely our hearts are pure and our intentions spotless when we are not solicitous of the opinion and censures of men, but only that what we do be our duty and accepted of God. For our eyes will certainly be fixed there from whence we expect our reward; and if we desire that God should approve us it is a Sign we do His work and expect Him our paymaster.

"He loves virtue for God's sake and its own, that loves and honours it wherever it is to be seen. But he that is envious or angry at a virtue that is not his own, at the perfection or excellency of his neighbour, is not covetous of the virtue, but of its reward and reputation; and then his intentions are polluted. It was a great ingenuity in Moses that wished all the people might be prophets; but if he had designed his own honour he would have prophesied alone. But he that desires only that the work of God and religion shall go on is pleased with it, whosoever is the instrument.

"If we are not solicitous concerning the instruments and means of our actions, but use those means which God hath laid before us with resignation, indifference, and thankfulness, it is a good sign that we are rather intent upon the end of God's glory than our own convenience or temporal satisfaction."

A Prayer

Almighty God, we thank Thee for voices that come from other worlds, bringing sweet music and saving gospels. We know Thy word when we hear it. There is none like it; that voice is as a mighty rushing wind from heaven. May we always listen for the voices from beyond, and reply to them with obedience and thankfulness. Thou hast set us in a great school: many are the teachers sent from God: Thou hast taught us on every scale and according to every method; Thou hast addressed Thyself to our understanding, and our love, and our conscience, and our immortality. In this great school we have had prophets, mighty men gifted with penetrating vision, charged with the thunders of eloquence, gentle souls that wept with us in our distress, mighty souls that could deliver us in our despair. If we have listened to common teachers when we might have listened to prophets, the good God of the prophets forgive us. Enable us always to listen only to the great, the tender, the wise, the sympathetic; may we shed off from us all weakness, frivolity, pettiness, and cry mightily after that which is sublime, divine. The Lord give us sight, clear and penetrating; the Lord give us eyes in our heart.

—Joseph Parker.

XIII.

MEDITATION AND ACTION

> I can do all things in Him that strengtheneth me.
> —*Paul.*

"NOW watch me burn out for God," said Henry Martyn. He had been talking with his Lord in the secret place until his soul burned within him. He had been quiet before God until his heart was aflame. Wise old Pythagoras knew the value of this quiet waiting, for he required each of his pupils to live for a year without once asking a question or making an explanation. But how infinitely more it means to the disciple of Jesus to wait quietly before his Lord. After such a waiting action is inevitable.

How can one who has talked with God and heard the voice of the unresting Christ do otherwise than go forward when he comes from the Presence Chamber? There is an atmosphere of resistless enthusiasm wherever the Son of God goes. His presence transforms every valley of dry bones into a living unconquerable army. It was one of Napoleon's veteran soldiers, a sergeant of the guard, to whom Napoleon was everything, who said to a newly enlisted man for whom he had formed a friendship, "The Emperor is come! The Emperor is here!" And the young soldier said, "How do you know, sergeant? I have just been down to the general's quarters and I have seen nothing of him." And the sergeant said: "Don't you see that all the world is up and stirring? You don't understand, but he is here. I feel it in the soles of my feet. When he is not here everything limps, but now, see down there! Everything is moving. Look at those expresses galloping along the road. The Emperor is come!" There is no loitering or limping where Jesus is. His presence transforms the hesitating soul into a hero, the sleeping host into a mighty army. You can always tell when the King has come.

Behind every successful life must be some great purpose. This is what Proclus the Athenian meant when he said, "Life is never at its best until it is caught in the upward sweep of some great enthusiasm." Such a purpose is usually born in the quiet place of meditation. In how many lives work becomes drudgery simply because behind the toil there is no high aim. That is not God's way for us. His plan is to sanctify every honourable occupation and have us perform daily duties with a consciousness of His presence, and for His glory.

> "Forenoon, and afternoon, and night;—Forenoon,
> And afternoon, and night; Forenoon, and—what?
> The empty song repeats itself. No more?
> Yea, that is life; make this forenoon sublime,
> This afternoon a psalm, this night a prayer,
> And time is conquered, and thy crown is won."

There are some things essential to the highest and noblest action. Foremost among these is peace. At first thought this may seem a paradox, but peace is not simply stillness. Dr. J. H. Jowett well says: "Peace is life, it is motion, it is movement without friction. We may find its fitting symbol in some great engine house when the monster is at work and every part coöperates with every other part in smooth and perfect communion. Peace is not found when every instrument in the orchestra is silent, but when every instrument is making its own contribution, and the result is rich and perfect harmony."

Now meditation takes the grit and sand from the axle, and makes the wheels of life run more smoothly. Meditation removes the discordant note from the orchestra and makes the music perfect. Meditation gives us a new consciousness of the presence of Him whom the winds and the sea obey, and so brings peace. It is the presence of Christ that eliminates worry and distraction from the life. "Peace," said Jesus, "I leave with you, My peace I give unto you: not as the world giveth, give I unto you. Let not your heart be troubled, neither let it be afraid." Where He is, peace abides. It is then that we do our best work.

Then, too, joy is essential to the noblest action. Henry Churchill King, speaking of the relation of joy to the will, puts it thus: "The relation is close and simple. Joy directly increases our vitality. Greater vitality gives greater sense of reality. This means stronger convictions. Of convictions purposes are born. And conviction and purpose make influence certain. . . . An ultimate message of hope is essential to the strongest living."

And herein may be found the reason why Jesus has so much to say about joy. With Him it is vital to aggressive Christian service. In spite of the strain of sadness—the sadness of farewell—that runs through that remarkable sixteenth chapter of St. John's Gospel, the note of joy is sounded loud and clear: "Ask and receive, that your joy may be full. . . . Your joy no man taketh from you. . . . Your sorrow shall be turned into joy. . . . In the world ye shall have tribulation: but be of good cheer I have overcome the world." A life filled with the joy of the Lord is almost certain to be a life of intensest activity in doing good. Paul knew this and, in his letters, so often exhorts his converts to "rejoice in the Lord." Indeed he declares that the kingdom of heaven is "righteousness and peace and *joy in the Holy Ghost*." And knowing Paul's ideals for the kingdom of God we must see how intimate in his mind was the relation between joy and action.

Then, too, love is necessary to the noblest action. Where all else fails love will win. Love will make opportunity. Love for God will keep the heart motive pure and the life clean. There is no motive power like love. It is irresistible. Nothing can stand before love—not even death.

> "Sink down ye separating hills!
> Let sin and death remove!
> 'Tis love that drives my chariot wheels,
> And death must yield to love."

Yonder in Northern India stand the two great cities of Lucknow and Cawnpore. Between them lies forty miles of densely populated country. Just before the terrible Sepoy rebellion broke out, a little English woman left her baby girl in charge of the nurse at the residency in Lucknow and went to Cawnpore to visit another English family. While she was there the rebellion broke like a cloudburst over all Northern India. Next morning after that first night of terror this little mother applied to the commanding officer in Cawnpore for a pass to Lucknow. The officer looked at her in amazement and said, "My poor woman, I cannot give you a pass to Lucknow. I couldn't get there myself with an army. Between here and there are one hundred and fifty thousand Sepoy fiends bent on the murder of every English resident." But the mother was not to be turned aside. She secured a native cart, and, disguised as a Hindoo woman, started at midnight for Lucknow. She threaded her way through the murderous crowds until she reached the gates of the city. Then it seemed as if her journey had only begun. General Havelock afterwards fought for three days in the streets before he reached the residency. But this brave little mother pushed her way through the frenzied throng until she came to the residency and clasped her child to her breast. What led that mother to defy death in its most horrible form? What, but love? There is no idle waiting where love is. There is no cowardice where love is.

But peace and joy and love thrive best when time is given to meditation upon the promises and goodness of God. It is then that the Holy Spirit has opportunity to speak to the soul, and pour out His gifts. It is then that He quickens and strengthens all these virtues and thus prepares us for the highest and noblest service. Savonarola waited in the quiet of the Brescian convent until peace and joy and love flooded his soul, and the presence of God so enriched and empowered his life, that the multitudes thronged to hear him, while princes and popes trembled at his words of fire.

A Prayer

Oh, Lord Jesus, Thou art nearer to me now than to Thy disciples in the days of Thy flesh!

> Closer to me than breathing,
> Nearer than hands and feet.

Thou art the constant friend, and Thou art the Light of the world. Then I shall walk steadily in Thy light. Then I shall not stumble or stray or lose my way. Thy company is better than that of princes, and Thy guidance surer than the stars. Unfalteringly would I keep step with Thee, even though the path Thou takest leads to the Garden and the Cross, knowing that Thou wilt lead at last to the daybreak that is eternal and the glory that is undimmed.

XIV.

HELPS TO MEDITATION

> Meditate upon these things:
> Give thyself wholly to them.
> —*Paul to Timothy.*

THE art of meditation must be learned. There is no possibility of stumbling upon it by chance. There is no royal course of ease to its gateway. Its blessed paths are trodden only by those who have toiled along many a tiresome road. But God, in His goodness, has provided so many helps for him who seeks this way that all who want to know its joy may do so.

There is one Companion and only one for the pathway of meditation, and that is the Holy Spirit. His company is indispensable. He knows the way and is ever willing to guide us. "Some place their religion in books," says Thomas à Kempis, "some in images, some in the pomp and splendour of external worship, but some with illuminated understandings heareth what the Holy Spirit speaketh in their hearts."

His mission is to reveal Christ and so open the eyes of our understanding that the crucified and risen Saviour shall be all in all to us. He makes us sensible, too, of the nearness and reality of the spiritual world. The more we have of the Spirit's companionship the more responsive we are to spiritual things. The eye sees more clearly the deep things of God, and the ear is more sensitive to the voice of God.

It is said that at the siege of Lucknow the first person to know of the near approach of the British troups, marching to the rescue of the city, was a little girl whose senses had become so keen through long illness that she heard the highland pipers while they were yet miles away. And he whose spiritual senses have been made keen by companionship with the Holy Spirit in hours of meditation and prayer will have such keenness of spiritual sight and hearing that he will sense victory from a distance, and will always recognize the earliest signs of gospel triumph.

The Holy Spirit makes use of the Bible in the hour of meditation. "Behold, I will pour out My Spirit unto you, I will make known My words unto you." "But when the Comforter is come," said Jesus, "which is the Holy Spirit, whom the Father will send in My name, He shall teach you all things, and bring all things to your remembrance, whatsoever I have said unto you." George Matheson, in his inimitable and devout way, says: "There are words lying in thy memory which are not yet revealed to thee—holy words, sacred words, words learned at a mother's knee, but whose beauty is by thee as yet unfelt, unseen. When the Spirit comes the old words will come to thee as something new. Thou shalt marvel at what thou hast passed by unnoticed on the way. Thou shalt wonder at the richness of the Lord's prayer, at the power of the Sermon on the Mount, at the tenderness of the story of a prodigal son. Thou shalt be surprised at the melody of old psalms, thrilled by the novelty of familiar incidents, stirred by the freshness of well-known passages. To him who is a new creature old things are all made new; the mind that was empty to the eye of sense, to the spirit reveals gold."

The Holy Spirit makes use of good books to enrich the hour of meditation. There are a number of spiritual classics which should be in the home of every growing Christian. Prominent among these is "The Imitation of Christ" by Thomas à Kempis. In spite of its deep note of pessimism and its dark pictures of this world, yet, outside the Bible, perhaps no other book has been such a permanent inspiration to real spiritual worship and heart devotion.

That was a beautiful tribute paid by George Eliot to this book when, in "The Mill on the Floss," she says:

"This small, old-fashioned book, for which you need pay only sixpence at a book-stall, *works miracles to this day*, turning bitter waters into sweetness: while expensive sermons and treatises, newly issued, leave all things as they were before. It was written down by a hand that waited for the heart's prompting; it is the chronicle of a solitary, hidden anguish, struggle, trust, and triumph—not written on velvet cushions to teach endurance to those who are treading with bleeding feet on the stones. And so it remains to all time a lasting record of human needs and human consolations; the voice of a brother who, ages ago, felt, suffered and renounced . . . with a fashion of speech different from ours, but under the same silent, far-off heavens, the same strivings, the same failures, the same weariness."

Every Christian home should have, if possible, a supply of these devotional books, a list of which can be secured from any religious publishing house, and a part of the quiet hour should be given to their perusal. It is to the shame of many Christian homes that one finds in the home library so much of the sentimental and trashy fiction of the day, and so little of the great classical spiritual literature of the centuries.

The Holy Spirit uses the biographies of godly men and women to make helpful the hour of meditation. In Auguste Comte's calendar he proposes that each day we should meditate on the life of some benefactor of humanity to whom that day's thoughts should be devoted. Here and there on the mountain peaks of Christian history have stood men and women of mighty faith in God, and to whom God has revealed Himself in wonderful power and blessing. To study these lives and meditate on their devotion and heroism will almost surely steady wavering feet and lift up hands that hang down.

Take, for instance, the life of John the Scot, who wrote, "There are as many unveilings of God as there are saintly souls." Living in the days of the Norse invaders, and when European civilization was at low ebb, this Irish scholar was "one of the torch bearers in the long line of teachers of mystical religion." His Christian polemics might be studied with great spiritual profit in our own day. Some things will be found that have upon them the mustiness of the darkened age in which he lived, but in many things he was far in advance of his time. His voice was lifted against the encroaching materialism and the corruption of the Church. He was condemned by church councils, and his writings confiscated, but he was one of God's own heroes. He was a voice crying in the wilderness and finding little response in those dark, dark days. "But there was in him," says one, "a loftiness of spirit, a boldness of vision, a virile idealism, which was sure to be an inspiration to many noble minds in later ages who were, as he was, consecrated to the service of the Invisible Church."

And the history of the Christian Church will be found to contain the record of many a noble life the study of which will greatly enrich the hours of meditation, and leave its permanent spiritual impress on the life.

A Prayer

And now, O Blessed Spirit, teach me the way of holy meditation! Then shall I have the open vision. I seem now so often to have to feel my way in the dark. Give me the undimmed eye of faith.

> I ask no dream, no prophet ecstasies,
> No sudden rending of this veil of clay;
> No angel visitant, no opening skies,
> But take the dimness of my soul away.

Too often spiritual things appear as mere shadows. May I begin to see that they are the great realities of life. Show me, O Lord, how to open the door of heavenly contemplation, and then, in the "secret of His presence," I shall come to know better the reality and authority of the spiritual. Make me a mystic in the highest and best sense of that much misunderstood word. May I come to know the hidden things of God. Thou hast said that "the secret of the Lord is with them that fear Him." Thou knowest, O Lord, that I fear Thee and love Thee. But I want to know Thee better and love Thee more. Therefore I wait at Thy feet, and plead for Thy mercy. Be gracious, Lord, even unto me, and "let the words of my mouth and the meditation of my heart be acceptable in Thy sight, O Lord, my strength and my redeemer."

www.ingramcontent.com/pod-product-compliance
Lightning Source LLC
Chambersburg PA
CBHW020430010526
44118CB00010B/512